CAMPBELL

3

For Your Information

Reading and Vocabulary Skills

SECOND EDITION

TEACHER'S MANUAL

with TESTS and ANSWER KEYS

by Nan Clarke

KAREN BLANCHARD CHRISTINE ROOT

For Your Information 3, Second Edition
Teacher's Manual with Tests and Answer Keys

Pearson Education, 10 Bank Street, White Plains, NY 10606

Staff credits: The people who made up the *For Your Information 3* team, representing editorial, production, design, and manufacturing, are Rhea Banker, Mindy DePalma, Christine Edmonds, Gosia Jaros-White, Laura Le Dréan, Linda Moser, Edith Pullman, Jane Townsend, Mykan White, and Pat Wosczyk.
Cover design: MADA Design, Inc.
Text font: 11/13 Times Roman
Text composition: Laserwords

ISBN-10: 0-13-243662-0
ISBN-13: 978-0-13-243662-5

Printed in the United States of America

CONTENTS

Scope and Sequence

UNIT	CHAPTER	READING SELECTION	READING SKILL
1 **CROSS-CULTURAL CONNECTIONS**	Chapter 1	Kissing Your Way Around the World	Identifying the Main Idea of a Paragraph
	Chapter 2	Communicating with Gestures	Using Background Knowledge
	Chapter 3	The Recipe for Success	Reading with a Purpose
abc NEWS **Video Excerpt:** Personal Space			
2 **MYSTERIES FROM THE PAST**	Chapter 1	The Mysterious Statues of Easter Island	Previewing and Predicting Making Inferences
	Chapter 2	The Nazca Lines	Skimming for the Main Idea Making Inferences Scaning for Information
	Chapter 3	Frozen in Time	Reading with a Purpose Making Inferences
abc NEWS **Video Excerpt:** Easter Island			
3 **MUSIC TO MY EARS**	Chapter 1	Musicians Who Make a Difference	Using Background Knowledge
	Chapter 2	Happy Birthday to a Musical Genius	Skimming for the Main Idea Identifying Facts and Opinions
	Chapter 3	The Power of Music	Previewing and Predicting Identifying Facts and Opinions Identifying the Main Idea of a Paragraph
abc NEWS **Video Excerpt:** Wynton Marsalis			
4 **GETTING DOWN TO BUSINESS**	Chapter 1	The Big Business of Fads	Using Graphic Organizers: Charts
	Chapter 2	The Price of Power	Skimming for the Main Idea Identifying Facts and Opinions
	Chapter 3	Smells Sell!	Using Background Knowledge Identifying Supporting Information
abc NEWS **Video Excerpt:** Teen Trends			

VOCABULARY SKILL	APPLICATION SKILL
Learning Synonyms	Reading an Interview Completing a Chart Taking a Survey Writing a Journal Entry
Understanding Word Parts: The Prefixes *il-, ir-, im-, and in-*	
Understanding Word Parts: The Suffix *–tion*	
Understanding Word Parts: The Prefix *co-*	Making a Time Capsule Doing Research Writing a Journal Entry
Learning Antonyms	
Using Context Clues Understanding Word Parts: The Suffixes *-ian* and *-ist*	
Learning Idioms: Expressions with *Make*	Making a CD Writing a Journal Entry
Learning Compound Words	
Learning Synonyms	
Learning Idioms: Expressions about Money and Business	Doing Research Writing a Journal Entry
Understanding Word parts: The Suffixes *-able* and *-ible*	
Using Context Clues Learning Idioms: Expressions with the Word *Smell*	

Scope and Sequence

UNIT	CHAPTER	READING SELECTION	READING SKILL
5 TUNE IN TO TV	Chapter 1	The Early Days and Beyond	Skimming for the Main Idea Scanning for Information Using Graphic Organizers: Making a Time Using Graphic Organizers: Making a Chart
	Chapter 2	Dora the Explorer Leads the Way	Previewing and Predicting
	Chapter 3	Reality TV	Using Graphic Organizers: Making a Chart
abcNEWS **Video Excerpt:** Baby TV			
6 SUPERSTITIONS	Chapter 1	It's Your Lucky Number	Using Background Knowledge Making Inferences Scanning Using Graphic Organizers: Making a Chart
	Chapter 2	Superstitious Athletes	Skimming for the Main Idea Using Graphic Organizers: Making a Chart Identifying Facts and Opinions
	Chapter 3	It's Jinxed!	Summarizing
abcNEWS **Video Excerpt:** The Pharaoh's Curse			
7 OUR FRAGILE PLANET	Chapter 1	One Family with the Earth	Using Background Knowledge Making Inferences
	Chapter 2	Our Endangered Wildlife	Previewing and Predicting Understanding Cause and Effect Summarizing
	Chapter 3	The Heat Is On!	Using Background Knowledge Understanding Chain Reactions Summarizing
abcNEWS **Video Excerpt:** The Eagles Return			
8 LIVING A LONG LIFE	Chapter 1	Discovering the Secrets to a Long Life	Using Background Knowledge Making Inferences
	Chapter 2	What Makes a Champion?	Identifying Facts and Opinions
	Chapter 3	Good News for the Aging Brain	Using Background Knowledge Making Inferences
abcNEWS **Video Excerpt:** Longevity Gene?			

VOCABULARY SKILL	APPLICATION SKILL
Learning Homonyms	Making a Chart Debating an Issue Taking a Survey Writing a Journal Entry
Understanding Word Parts: The Prefixes *multi-* and *bi-*	
Understanding Word Parts: The Suffixes *-ship* and *-ness*	
Learning Homonyms	Making a Chart Doing Research Writing a Newspaper Story Writing a Journal Entry
Learning Synonyms and Antonyms	
Using Context Clues Learning Synonyms and Antonyms	
Learning Homonyms	Reading a Speech Making a Poster Writing a Journal Entry
Understanding Word Parts: The Prefix *micro-*	
Using *Therefore* and *Because* Learning Synonyms and Antonyms	
Understanding Word Parts: Root Words; The Suffix *-ology*	Making a Poster Reading a Graph Writing a Journal Entry
Learning Idioms: Parts of the Body	
Three-Word Verbs	

INTRODUCTION

The FYI Approach

Welcome to *For Your Information,* a reading and vocabulary skill-building series for English language learners. The FYI series is based on the premise that students are able to read at a higher level of English than they can produce. An important goal of the texts is to help students move beyond passive reading to become active, thoughtful, and confident readers of English.

Each level in the series is tailored to focus on the specific needs of students to increase their vocabulary base and build their reading skills. In addition to comprehension and vocabulary practice activities, reading and vocabulary-building skills are presented throughout each chapter. Although FYI is a reading series, students also practice speaking, listening, and writing throughout the texts. In trademark FYI style, the tasks in all books are varied, accessible, and inviting, and they provide stimuli for frequent interaction.

The Second Edition

This popular series is now in its second edition. The book numbers have changed in the new edition and include the following levels:

For Your Information 1 Beginning
For Your Information 2 High-Beginning
For Your Information 3 Intermediate
For Your Information 4 High-Intermediate

The second edition of *For Your Information 3* features:

- new and updated reading selections
- designated target vocabulary words for study and practice
- expanded activities for building reading skills
- vocabulary building skills and "word-attack" activities
- a companion DVD of ABC News excerpts on related themes, with accompanying activities
- a glossary of target vocabulary words used in the readings

Teaching *For Your Information*

COMPONENTS

Each level of the FYI series includes a student book, a teacher's manual, which includes eight unit tests, an audio CD with recordings of the readings, and a DVD of related excerpts from ABC News programs.

STUDENT BOOK

Each student book in the FYI series contains eight thematically based units. The themes have universal appeal and allow for natural recycling of vocabulary and content.

UNIT FORMAT

All units open with a page of art and activities that introduce the theme. This is followed by three chapters with one reading each, a review section called *Tie It All Together*, and a Vocabulary Self-Test.

UNIT INTRODUCTION

The one-page introduction to each unit provides students with opportunities to review what they already know about the topic and uses related vocabulary that they already know in English. This page always includes a visual prompt such as a photo or cartoon. Since this art sets the stage for the whole unit, make sure students use it as a springboard for discussion or vocabulary reinforcement. The page also includes several *Points to Ponder* questions designed to activate background knowledge and provide a framework for a student-generated discussion of the theme. To this end, the questions are intended to encourage students to personalize the information and bring their own experiences into the discussion.

THE CHAPTERS

Each unit consists of three separate chapters. Each chapter is built on a reading passage directly related to the theme of the unit. All readings are either authentic or adapted from authentic sources. The variety of sources, including magazine and newspaper articles, interviews, the Internet, and works of fiction, nonfiction, and poetry, expose students to the wide range of writing styles they may expect to encounter in their everyday lives.

Specific reading and vocabulary skills, called *Skills for Success*, are presented in each chapter. Fluent reading involves a combination of specific reading skills (e.g., predicting, skimming for main ideas, scanning for specific information, identifying main and supporting ideas, distinguishing between facts and opinions) which can be identified, practiced, and evaluated. Most second-language learners benefit from explicit instruction in these skills. This involves giving the skill a name, explaining why the skill is helpful, describing how to use the skill effectively, and providing practice in using it. The specific skills are recycled throughout the text to give students practice using them in a variety of contexts. The *Skills for Success* also include vocabulary-building strategies and "word-attack" skills, such as understanding word parts, learning synonyms and antonyms, organizing words, understanding phrasal verbs, and inferring meaning from context. In addition, general language and learning strategies (organizing information, taking notes, making charts, etc.) are included throughout chapters to enhance students' ability to comprehend, evaluate, and remember information. Finally, real-life skills such as using maps, reading menus, recognizing common signs and symbols, interpreting graphs, etc., are interspersed throughout the series.

Reflecting our philosophy that reading is an interactive process, the chapters have three main sections: *Before You Read*, *Reading*, and *After You Read*.

Before You Read

Since successful activation of background knowledge has been shown to greatly enhance the reading experience, each chapter begins with a *Before You Read* section that serves to get students thinking about what they already know about the topic of the reading. The first activity is usually done with a partner to encourage collaborative learning. The second activity introduces the target vocabulary that students will encounter in the passage. Vocabulary words and phrases that are essential to understanding the passage are presented before the reading in order to improve students' comprehension and fluency as they read.

Reading

The reading in each chapter is related to the overall theme of the unit, allowing students to explore the theme in depth. All of the reading passages were chosen with the idea in mind that students relate better to high-interest texts that present real information.

After You Read

This section includes comprehension exercises and vocabulary practice. A variety of exercise types are used to reflect the different styles of students. Students can work alone, in pairs, or in small groups to complete these exercises. The reading comprehension exercises test recall and understanding. They often require students to employ a specific reading skill to complete the task. For example, if students have learned the skill of recognizing time order, they might be expected to number events from the reading so they are in the correct time order.

The Vocabulary Practice includes several exercises. The first is designed to test word meanings in the context of the reading, and the second challenges students to use the vocabulary in new contexts. These are followed by the presentation of a specific vocabulary skill that students practice and must use in order to complete the remaining vocabulary exercises.

Talk It Over This section provides students with an opportunity to talk about the topic of the reading in pairs, in small groups, or as a class. The questions are designed to motivate learners to relate the reading to their own experiences. Students are encouraged to share their opinions and bring their own experiences into the discussion.

Expansion Activities Many chapters include an additional expansion activity that encourages students to expand on their real-life skills such as reading help-wanted ads, using charts and graphs, and doing research. Other expansion activities are designed to allow students to interact with each other by conducting surveys, holding debates, and completing collaborative hands-on projects (making posters, cookbooks, etc.).

FYIs These are pieces of information related to the unit theme that are interspersed throughout the text.

Tie It All Together Each unit concludes with a section called *Tie It All Together* that returns to the general theme of the unit. This section has five parts: *Discussion*, *Just for Fun*, *Video Activity*, *Reader's Journal*, and *Vocabulary Self-Test*.

Discussion The discussion questions in this section are more open-ended than those in the chapters. Students should be encouraged to feel free to express their opinions about the topics they have read about. The questions can also be used for writing prompts or class debates.

Just for Fun The Just for Fun activities provide enjoyable ways for students to use the language they have learned in the unit. The activities include crossword puzzles, games, and word searches.

Video Activity The video activity is built around a short segment from ABC News that is related to the unit topic. Teachers should preview the video before showing it and create previewing questions that activate prior knowledge. Before showing the video to the students, go over the meanings of the vocabulary items and discuss any additional words and expressions that may interfere with comprehension.

Reader's Journal A Reader's Journal at the end of each unit integrates reading and writing and helps students reflect in a non-threatening format on what they have read. The purpose of the writing task is to encourage students to reflect on, synthesize, and react to the ideas they have read about and discussed in the unit. Specific topics are provided as prompts for journal entries, but students are free to write about anything they want.

Vocabulary Self-Test The Vocabulary Self-Test at the end of each unit tests students on the target words presented at the beginning of each reading. Students should be encouraged to check their answers in the answer key and monitor their own progress.

UNIT TESTS

The Unit Tests, which are found at the back of this Teacher's Manual, consist of readings related to each unit theme, followed by questions that test comprehension as well as reading and vocabulary skills presented in the corresponding Student Book unit. These tests should be given after work on the unit is completed.

UNIT-by-UNIT
TEACHING TIPS

UNIT 1 CROSS-CULTURAL CONNECTIONS

Theme: In Unit 1, students explore two ways in which cultures are often distinct: gestures and food.

Readings: The readings in this unit examine topics that highlight some interesting cultural differences: the custom of kissing in various cultures, gestures and their meanings in different cultures, and flavors that characterize a variety of ethnic food.

Skills for Success: Identifying the Main Idea of a Paragraph, Learning Synonyms, Using Background Knowledge, Understanding Word Parts: The Prefixes *il-*, *ir-*, *im-*, and *in-*, Reading with a Purpose, and Understanding Word Parts: The Suffix-*tion*

Vocabulary:

appreciation	deal	ill	signifies
associated with	documents	instead of	system
attractive	ethnic	make up	unreliable
authority	extensive	passed down	vary
complicated	flavorings	represent	
cuisine	generation	rude	

Points to Ponder

After students have answered the questions on page 1, ask them to share any other significant customs of classroom behavior in their culture.

Chapter 1: Kissing Your Way Around the World (pages 2–7)

Reading

This reading discusses the significance of kissing in various cultures and historical information about the custom of kissing.

After You Read

After students complete exercise A on page 4, have them work in small groups and answer these questions:

1. What are the customs for kissing people in your country?
   a. Do you kiss your relatives when you visit them?
   b. Do you kiss your friends when you meet them?
   c. Is it polite to kiss someone in public places?
2. What are some other kissing customs in your country?

SKILL FOR SUCCESS: Identifying the Main Idea of a Paragraph

- Tell students that reading material is often divided into paragraphs. This type of organization helps the writer to present the information clearly and it helps the reader to easily understand what the reading is about.

- Point out that each paragraph includes a main idea, or what the paragraph is about. Main ideas are often the first or last sentence in the paragraph.
- Have students reread the first paragraph in the reading on page 3 and point out what the main idea is (*kissing customs differ around the world*).
- Tell students that the other sentences in a paragraph are supporting details that give more information to the main idea. Have the class identify the supporting details in the first paragraph in the reading. Write them on the board. (*What are specific customs for kissing people in your country? Do you kiss relatives or friends when you see them? Is it polite to kiss in public? Kissing customs depend on where you live.*)
- Have students work in groups and identify the main ideas and the supporting details in the other paragraphs in the reading.
- Have students complete Exercise B on page 5.

EXTRA PRACTICE:

- Find a four- or five-paragraph reading suitable for the class and cut it up into single paragraphs.
- Divide the class into groups and give each group one paragraph from the reading.
- Ask groups to write the main idea of their paragraph on the chalkboard or new print pad.
- Have the group make a list of details that support the main idea in that paragraph.
- Have the class work together to put the paragraphs in correct order.

SKILL FOR SUCCESS: Learning Synonyms

- Tell students that a valuable source for learning synonyms is a good dictionary.
- Have students complete Exercise C on page 7.

EXTRA PRACTICE:

- After students have completed Exercise C on page 7, have them reread the first paragraph on page 3 and find synonyms for these words:

  family (*relatives*) general (*universal*) traditions (*customs*)
- Have students use the synonyms in original sentences and share the sentences with the class by writing them on the board or newsprint pad.

Chapter 2: Communicating with Gestures (pages 8–14)

SKILL FOR SUCCESS: Using Background Knowledge

- Tell students that using background knowledge is a skill that we use often in life. Using what we already know about something can enrich our understanding in new situations. For example, if we frequently use the drive-through window of a particular restaurant, when we go to a drive-through restaurant we've never been to before, we use what we know to place and order and purchase our food. We know that we'll hear someone ask us what we want through a speaker, we'll place our order, and they'll tell us how much it is.

Then we'll drive forward to a window and pay for our food. So we already know that before we pull up to the speaker, we should look at the menu and decide what we want. When we pull up to the window, we should have our money ready and be prepared to take the food into the car.

- Have students respond to this question:

  What are some other areas in your life in which you use what you already know to understand something new?

Reading

This selection is about a variety of human gestures and their meanings in different cultures.

After You Read

After students have completed Exercises A, B, and C on pages 11–12, divide the class into small groups. Have groups go back to the reading on pages 9–10 and look at the list of twenty gestures presented there. Have students discuss which of these gestures are common in their countries and what they mean.

SKILL FOR SUCCESS: Understanding Word Parts: The Prefixes *il-, ir-, im-, and in-*

Point out that with this particular group of prefixes, each one changes the base word to mean its opposite. For example, the base word *literate* with the prefix *il-* becomes *illiterate* and means *not literate.* Clarify that these particular prefixes are not used with every word.

EXTRA PRACTICE:

- After students have completed Exercises C and D on page 13 and checked their answers, have them work in pairs and use these prefixes to write the opposite of these words:

  accessible (*inaccessible*)
  credible (*incredible*)
  flexible (*inflexible*)
  logical (*illogical*)
  probable (*improbable*)
  proper (*improper*)
  rational (*irrational*)

- Then have them use the new words in original sentences and share their sentences with another pair.

Chapter 3: The Recipe for Success (pages 15–20)

SKILL FOR SUCCESS: Reading with a Purpose

Ask students to explain what it means to read with a goal in mind. Encourage students to give examples of the questions a person may ask about a reading. Then have them complete Exercise B on page 15.

Reading

This reading is an interview about certain flavors that are associated with specific world cultures.

After You Read

After students complete Exercises A and B on page 17, have them talk about the different flavorings people use in their countries and specific dishes in which they are used. Have them describe the dishes in detail.

SKILL FOR SUCCESS: Understanding Word Parts: The Suffix *-tion.*

- Ask students what the difference is between a prefix and suffix.
- Tell students that the suffix *-tion* cannot be added to every verb.
- Emphasize that adding the suffix *-tion* changes the way a word is used and that there are often spelling changes when the suffix is added.
- Have students complete Exercise C on pages 18–19.

EXTRA PRACTICE:

- Have students look up definitions for these verbs and then change them to nouns.

communicate (*communication*)	converse (*conversation*)	represent (*representation*)
connect (*connection*)	produce (*production*)	vary (*variation*)

- Have students use each noun in an original sentence and share their sentences with the class by putting them on the board or newsprint pad.

Unit 1: Tie It All Together

Just for Fun

- Make a cookbook. Have each student write a recipe for a dish that is typical in his/her own country. Make copies of each recipe and then collate and staple them into a cookbook.
- Have an international buffet. Ask each student to prepare a dish from his/her country and bring it to class. Bon appetit!

Video Activity: *Personal Space*

Do your own experiment with personal space. Here are some ideas:

1. Visit a food court, cafeteria, or other public eating place where people seat themselves. Watch how people space themselves. Especially notice people who are alone. How far do people sit from strangers? Write down your observations and share them with your class.
2. Visit a food court, cafeteria, or other public eating place where people seat themselves. Choose a place to sit that is closer to strangers than you would normally choose. How do you feel? What are you thinking? Do the people near you notice you or talk to you? What do they say? Make notes about your experience and share them with your class.
3. You can try this one with a friend if you don't want to try it alone. Visit a food court, cafeteria, or other public eating place where people seat themselves. Look around for a table where there is space for one or two more people to sit. Ask the people at the table if you can sit with them. What happens? What do they say? How do you feel? What do you say? Do they include you in their conversation or ignore you? Make notes about your experience and share them with your class.

UNIT 2 MYSTERIES FROM THE PAST

Theme: In Unit 2, students explore three intriguing creations from long ago.

Readings: The readings in each of the three chapters examine a different ancient mystery: the statues of Easter Island; the Nazca lines of Peru; and Otzi, the oldest human body ever found in Europe.

Skills for Success: Previewing and Predicting, Making Inferences, Learning Word Parts: The Prefix *co-*, Skimming for the Main Idea, Scanning for Information, Learning Antonyms, Reading with a Purpose, Using Context Clues, Learning Word Parts: The Suffixes *-ian* and *-ist*

Vocabulary:

agriculture	descendant	intrigues	sparked
baffled	disasters	magnificent	speculate
belongings	estimated	on purpose	theory
biologists	evidence	sensation	tiny
carve	fascinate	shocked	violence
cooperated	figure out	silent	weapons

Points to Ponder

Before students begin this unit, bring in a large world map and hang it on the wall. Place map pins or map flags to identify the Easter Islands, Peru, and the Otzal Alps between Italy and Austria. After students have discussed the questions on page 25, ask the class to talk about some of the amazing things they know about that were built by ancient people. Ask students to identify the locations and mark them on the world map.

Chapter 1: The Mysterious Statues of Easter Island (pages 26–33)

Before You Read

After the pair work in exercise A, ask the students to call out the words they used to describe the statues in response to question 2 and have someone write them on the board. Make corrections in spelling and pronunciation as needed.

SKILL FOR SUCCESS: Previewing and Predicting

- Ask students:

  What does the prefix *pre-* mean? (*before*)

  What do the words *preview* and *predict* mean? (*look or see before; guess or say what will happen before it occurs*)

  In what places do previews typically take place? (*movie theaters, museums*)

  Who are some people that predict things? (*weather forecasters*)

  How does a weather forecaster make predictions? (*by using guesses based on information/facts: temperature, clouds in the sky,* etc.)

- A good reader can also make predictions based on information. A reader can get information by previewing titles, subtitles, headings, pictures, captions, and words in bold or italic print.

Reading

This reading is about the mysterious statues on Easter Island, a small island in the southern part of the Pacific Ocean.

After You Read

FYI: Easter Island belongs to Chile and is one of the most isolated inhabited islands in the world.

SKILL FOR SUCCESS: Making Inferences

- Point out to students that we are always making inferences based on information we get from everything around us. When we see a lot of cars in the supermarket parking lot, we infer the supermarket is busy. When we observe a couple laughing and talking in a restaurant, we infer that they are having a good time.
- Ask students to share some everyday situations in which they make inferences based on another person's behavior or tone of voice, or a situation they observe.
- Have students complete Exercise C on page 30.

SKILL FOR SUCCESS: The Prefix *co-*

Point out that like the prefix *pre-,* the prefix *co-* is often separated from the base word by a hyphen. In many cases, it is a matter of style, chosen by a publisher or institution. A good rule to follow is: Use a hyphen when forming nouns, adjectives, and verbs that indicate occupation or status; do not hyphenate in other combinations: coauthor, coworker, coeducational, cocurricular, and cooperate. Dictionaries may also vary in their use of the hyphen with these prefixes.

EXTRA PRACTICE: As an additional activity, have students work alone or in pairs to come up with a list of five or six words that they think might use the prefix *co-,* and have them consult a dictionary to confirm their guesses.

Chapter 2: The Nazca Lines (pages 34–40)

Before You Read

After students have answered the questions on page 34, ask if anyone has ever heard about or seen the Nazca Lines. Ask those students to share what they know with the class.

SKILL FOR SUCCESS: Skimming for the Main Idea

- Introduce this skill by reminding students that in the last unit they worked on identifying the main idea of a paragraph. Good readers also learn to skim, or read quickly, for the main idea of the entire article that they are reading.
- Tell students that when skimming, they will not read word for word. Instead, they will move their eyes quickly through the reading for clues about the topic. Skimming focuses on getting the "big picture," not specific details.

EXTRA PRACTICE: Find three readings that are three to four paragraphs each and at a level appropriate for the class. Distribute a copy of one reading to each student. Give them a limited time to skim the article and write one sentence that expresses the main idea of the reading. Do the same for the other two readings. When students have skimmed all three and written a sentence for each one, have them work in pairs or small groups to compare their answers.

Reading

This reading is about the curious line drawings in the Nazca desert of Peru that can be seen only from the air. Some of the lines that make up these drawings are as long as nine miles.

SKILL FOR SUCCESS: Scanning for Information

- Ask students what they think scanning is. (*to read quickly for specific information*)
- Point out to students that scanning is a skill we often use in everyday life. For example, we might scan an ad for a movie to find out who the actors are. If we walk into a crowded restaurant, we scan the room until we find the person we are meeting.

EXTRA PRACTICE: Have students return to the reading from Chapter 1 on page 27. Give them one minute to scan the reading and write down as many numbers as they can find.

SKILL FOR SUCCESS: Learning Antonyms

An excellent website for finding both antonyms and synonyms is: www.synonym.com.

EXTRA PRACTICE:

- Have students work in pairs to find antonyms for these vocabulary words from Unit 1.

attractive (*unattractive*)	extensive (*scarce*)	rude (*polite*)
complicated (*simple*)	ill (*healthy*)	unreliable (*reliable*)

- Have students use each of the antonyms in an original sentence and share their work with another pair.

Chapter 3: Frozen in Time (pages 41–48)

Reading

This selection is about the discovery of the body of a person who lived more than 5,000 years ago and the mystery of his life and death.

After You Read

Ask students to look at the questions they wrote in Before You Read, Exercise B on page 41. Have students work in pairs and discuss their questions and the answers they found. If students have unanswered questions, they can do an Internet search on Otzi to find answers to their questions and report their findings to the class.

SKILL FOR SUCCESS: Using Context Clues

Point out to students that using context clues to gain understanding or meaning is a skill that they already use regularly. We are always looking at clues in the world around us to find meaning. We can walk into a roomful of people and look for clues about what they are doing there. How are they dressed? Are they interacting with one another? What are their facial expressions? Are they eating or drinking? Are they wearing name tags? What are they doing? Transferring this skill to reading is simply a matter of looking for different clues.

SKILL FOR SUCCESS: Learning Word Parts: The Suffixes *-ian* and *-ist*

EXTRA PRACTICE:

- Have students complete the chart below. They may use dictionaries if needed.

Suffix	Job	Clue
-ist		plays the piano
-ist		studies science
-ian		practices politics
-ist		works with technology
-ian		studies mathematics

- Then have students work in pairs to write a question for which the jobs would be the correct answer. Students can use the questions in Exercise E on page 48 as a model. Have each pair write their questions on a clean sheet of paper, exchange papers with another pair, and work together to answer the new questions.

Unit 2: Tie It All Together

For Further Study

- Divide the class into seven groups and give each group one of the Seven Wonders of the Ancient World to research and report on to the class. They are:
  The Great Pyramid of Giza
  The Hanging Gardens of Babylon
  The Statue of Zeus at Olympia
  The Temple of Artemis at Ephesus
  The Mausoleum at Halicarnassus
  The Colossus of Rhodes
  The Lighthouse of Alexandria

- As a guide, students can answer these questions:
  What is the name of the ancient wonder?
  Where is it?
  Who created it?
  What is mysterious about it?
  What other significant information did you find about it?

Video Activity: *Easter Island*

Add these words to the list of words for study in Part A, page 50, of the Student Book:

clambered	incubator	majestic	peek

For Further Discussion

No one knows who the statues of Easter Island represent or why they were moved to the shoreline. What do people in your culture think or know about the statues of Easter Island? Work in a small group and share what you know about Easter Island or make up your own story about who the statues represent and how they were moved. Share your stories with the class.

UNIT 3 MUSIC TO MY EARS

Theme: Unit 3 highlights profiles of some famous musicians and the influence that music has in today's culture.

Readings: The readings in this unit introduce three popular musicians and their work for charity and humanitarian causes; the 250th birthday celebrations of Wolfgang Amadeus Mozart; and a description of how music affects people's behavior.

Skills for Success: Using Background Knowledge, Learning Idioms: Expressions with *Make,* Skimming for the Main Idea, Identifying Facts and Opinions, Learning Compound Words, Previewing and Predicting, Identifying the Main Idea of a Paragraph, and Learning Synonyms

Vocabulary:

accomplished	clients	humanitarian	praised
annoying	committed	inspirational	overcome
calming	composers	kick off	renovated
causes	delighted	lively	solo
celebrity	essential	masterpieces	victims
charities	genius	patient	

Points to Ponder

Add these questions to those on page 53:

- Who are some of your favorite musicians or groups?
- What do you like about them?

Chapter 1: Musicians Who Make a Difference (pages 54–59)

Reading

This article focuses on three modern musicians who are committed to making the world a better place: Irish rock star Bono; Puerto Rican pop star Ricky Martin; and British star Sting.

SKILL FOR SUCCESS: Learning Idioms: Expressions with *Make*

Remind students that an idiom is a group of words that, as a whole, have a meaning very different from each of the individual words.

EXTRA PRACTICE:

- Create a list of other idioms with *make* and a sentence for each idiom.
- Write each idiom on individual slips of paper. On separate pieces of paper, write the sentences that use each idiom. You can also visit www.geocities.com on the Internet and download the page of idioms with *make*. Print out the page and then cut the left column from the right column, and then cut each individual item so that you have 32 slips of paper—16 idioms and 16 sentences.
- Put the sentences in one basket and the idioms in another.
- Divide the class into two groups. Have each person in one group pick a slip of paper from the idiom basket. Have each person in the second group pick one slip from the sentence basket. (You may have to make adjustments for larger or smaller classes).
- Have the students in the idiom group mingle with students from the sentence group to find the sentence that uses the idiom they have.
- When each person finds "the match," have each pair write the sentence on the board and write a definition underneath the sentence. Review the sentences and definitions as a class.

Just for Fun

Have a dance party. Invite students to bring in music that accompanies a traditional dance from their native country. Students who bring in music can provide the group with information about the dance (origins, regions or groups where it is popular, and so on) and give a short dance lesson. Serve some snacks and soft drinks and have fun!

Chapter 2: Happy Birthday to a Musical Genius (pages 60–65)

Reading

This selection tells about the 250th birthday celebration of Wolfgang Amadeus Mozart, the Austrian musical genius who began composing at the age of five.

SKILL FOR SUCCESS: Identifying Facts and Opinions

- Before looking at the definitions of *fact* and *opinion* on page 62, write *fact* on one side of the board and *opinion* on the other. Elicit synonyms for or phrases associated with each. Ask for examples of each. (She has brown, curly hair versus She has beautiful hair; He makes $10,000 a year versus He doesn't make very much money.)
- Have students look at the definitions of *fact* and *opinion*. Spend some time talking about **why** it is important to understand the difference:

  It is natural to interpret events and form opinions about what goes on around us.

It is important to distinguish between fact and opinion so that we can understand the difference between information and a writer's **interpretation** of that information.

Understanding this distinction is essential to our understanding of what we are reading.

SKILL FOR SUCCESS: Learning Compound Words

EXTRA PRACTICE:

- Divide students into groups of three or four and give each group three or four of the compound words from this list found in Units 1 and 2:

anything	blackboard	fingernail	overcome
background	cookbook	handshake	someone
bearskin	eyelid	outsider	something

- Have each group find a definition for the words and then create an original sentence for each word. Have students write their sentences on the board. As a class, review the sentences and have students guess the meanings of each compound word. The group that worked with the word can confirm the guesses and provide definitions where needed.

Chapter 3: The Power of Music (pages 66–72)

Reading

This selection is about some of the research that has been done about the effects of music on people's behavior and about Muzak, a company that specializes in providing background music for businesses all over the world.

After You Read

After students have completed Exercise A on page 69, have them return to Exercise B, Previewing and Predicting, on pages 66–67 and look at the items they checked. Were their predictions accurate?

SKILL FOR SUCCESS: Learning Synonyms

EXTRA PRACTICE:

- Have students visit the website www.synonym.com, or use a dictionary or thesaurus to find synonyms for the underlined words from Chapters 1 and 2:

  He began his solo career . . .

  Sting is also dedicated to protecting the environment . . .

  We were delighted that it fell to Sydney Symphony . . .

  . . . he is especially devoted to helping communities

  Mozart would have existed without Salzburg

  He has also helped the victims of the tsunami . . .

  . . . his work for humanitarian causes has also earned him respect . . .

- Then have students write original sentences using the synonyms they found.

Talk It Over

EXTRA ACTIVITY: Ask students to visit a public building or office where background music is played and report to the class on the following:

- What kind of building or office did they visit?
- What kind of background music was played?
- How was that kind of music related to what was happening in the building?
- Did people seem to be aware of the music?

Unit 3: Tie It All Together

Video Activity: *Wynton Marsalis*

Before students begin the Video Activity, ask students to share what they know about jazz.

FYI: Jazz is popular music that originated in New Orleans, Louisiana, in the late nineteenth century. It is characterized by improvisation—performed without any preparation or written music. It is also known for its syncopation, which changes the rhythm of the music by accenting the weak beat.

UNIT 4 GETTING DOWN TO BUSINESS

Theme: In Unit 4, students look at the business world from three unique perspectives.

Readings: The reading selections in this unit include a highlight of some fad products that made their creators wealthy, international trends in developing alternative power sources, and the use of specific smells in retail sales.

Skills for Success: Using Graphic Organizers: Charts, Learning Idioms: Expressions about Money and Business, Skimming for the Main Idea, Identifying Facts and Opinions, Understanding Word Parts: The Suffixes *-able* and *-ible,* Using Background Knowledge, Identifying Supporting Information, Using Context Clues, Learning Idioms: Expressions with the Word *Smell*

Vocabulary:

alternative	fragrance	practical	tricky
catches on	fuel	proof	vehicle
convert	invested	run out of	volunteers
entice	led by the nose	sold like hotcakes	word of mouth
fake	made a mint	stinks	
flexible	mood	tips	

Points to Ponder

Add this question to the exercise on page 77:

Do people in your native country trust businesses and companies? Why or why not?

Chapter 1: The Big Business of Fads (pages 78–84)

Before You Read

Add these questions to the Exercise A on page 78:

What are some fad items that are (or were) popular in your country?

Why do you think they became popular?

Reading

Some lucky inventors have made millions from products they created. This selection features six fad items that were popular for a short time, but made their creators wealthy for life.

SKILL FOR SUCCESS: Using Graphic Organizers: Charts

Point out to students that charts are a common type of graphic organizer that we frequently encounter. Ask them for some examples of charts they have used in their lives. Some of them are various types of schedules, directions on over-the-counter medicines, graphs in newspaper articles, and menus in restaurants. Graphic organizers are useful because they help us arrange information in a simple, visual way. Visual learners often benefit from using charts.

EXTRA PRACTICE:

- After students have completed vocabulary exercises A and B on pages 82 and 83, have them work in pairs to make a chart with the vocabulary words from this chapter.

vocabulary item	definition	part of speech	example sentence

- Model the task using *catch on.* On the board, write the four headings. Then write *catch on* under the heading *vocabulary item.* Ask students what *catch on* means and write that on the board under the heading *definition.* Then ask what part of speech *catch on* is, and write that on the board under the heading *part of speech.* Ask the class to create an original sentence using *catch on,* and write that on the board under the heading *example sentence.*

SKILL FOR SUCCESS: Learning Idioms: Expressions about Money and Business

EXTRA PRACTICE:

- Give students the following idioms that relate to money and business and their definitions:

at all costs	at any expense of time, effort, or money
to be born with a silver spoon in one's mouth	to be born to wealth and comfort; to be born rich
to clean up	to make a lot of money; to make a big profit
a hard sell	a very aggressive or high-pressure way to sell something
monkey business	nonsense; ridiculous behavior
none of your business	of no concern to you

- Have students work in pairs to come up with a situation in which the idiom might be used.
- Have pairs write original sentences using each idiom.
- Have each pair write two sentences on the board.
- Review as a class and correct as needed.

Chapter 2: The Price of Power (pages 85–91)

Before You Read

Add these questions to Exercise A on page 85:

> What are some other energy sources that you have heard about or are used in your native country? How are they used?

Reading

This reading presents some alternative and creative solutions for using renewable energy sources.

After You Read

- After students have completed Exercise A on pages 87–88, have them work in pairs or small groups to create a chart based on information for the reading, using these headings:

Energy Source	Type of Energy Produced	Uses

- Have them write the charts on newsprint paper and hang them around the room.

SKILL FOR SUCCESS: Understanding Word Parts: The Suffixes *-able* and *-ible*

EXTRA PRACTICE:

- After students have completed Exercise C on page 90 and checked their answers, have them work individually to make adjectives from the following verbs (they may use dictionaries for help with spelling):

achieve (*achievable*) | observe (*observable*) | suggest (*suggestible*)
adjust (*adjustable*) | permit (*permissible*) | vary (*variable*)

- Have students check their work in pairs and then create an original sentence for each adjective.
- Have each pair join another pair to share their work.
- Have each group write one of the sentences on the board.
- Review with the class and correct as needed.

Chapter 3: Smells Sell! (pages 92–100)

Reading

This selection explores the use of smells by retailers to increase sales and some controversy about the ethics of using fragrances in this way.

FYI: Vanilla, a common flavoring used in foods, is a major ingredient in many perfumes; the Body Shop has begun selling a pure vanilla fragrance.

After You Read

After students have completed Exercise A on pages 94–95, have them look again at their answers for Before You Read, Exercise B on page 92. Were their guesses correct? What new information did they learn?

SKILL FOR SUCCESS: Identifying Supporting Information

EXTRA PRACTICE:

1.

- After students have completed Exercise B on pages 95–96 and have checked their answers, have them work in pairs and look at each sentence that they have identified as supporting information.
- Have them decide whether each sentence states a fact, provides a reason, or gives an example.
- Have each pair join another pair and compare their answers.
- Discuss the answers as a class.

2.

- Find a six- to seven-paragraph level-appropriate reading and cut it into individual paragraphs.
- Divide the class into groups—one group for each paragraph of the reading.
- Have each group identify the sentence that expresses the main idea in their paragraph and then label each of the other sentences as one that states a fact, provides a reason, or gives an example.
- Discuss each paragraph as a class.

SKILL FOR SUCCESS: Learning Idioms: Expressions with the Word *Smell*

EXTRA PRACTICE

- Add this idiom to the list at the beginning of Exercise E on page 99:
  to smell to high heaven: to be of very poor quality; suspicious or not reputable
  —His financial schemes smell to high heaven; I'm sure they're dishonest.
- Ask students if they know of any other idioms using the word *smell* and write them on the board. Discuss their meanings as a class and create examples of sentences using the idioms. For example:
  —*I smell where you're stepping* means I understand the direction of your thought (I get your drift).
  —*Smell out* means detect.
- Have students work in pairs to create an original dialogue using the idioms listed at the beginning of Exercise E on page 99 and any additional idioms with *smell* they have come up with (they can use the dialogue in Exercise E as a model).
- Have each pair perform the dialogue for the class.

Unit 4: Tie It All Together

FYI: The use of different smells is also popular in alternative medicine. **Aromatherapy,** commonly associated with complementary and alternative medicine, uses liquid plant materials or essential oils and other aromatic compounds from plants to affect someone's mood or health.

UNIT 5 TUNE IN TO TV

Theme: Unit 5 gives a brief history of TV and provides discussion about how TV both reflects and influences society.

Readings: The reading selections offer the history of TV; a look at *Dora the Explorer,* a children's TV show that features Latino characters; and a discussion about one of the most recent trends in television programming, reality TV.

Skills for Success: Skimming for Main Idea, Scanning for Information, Using Graphic Organizers: Making a Timeline, Learning Homonyms, Using Graphic Organizers: Making a Chart, Previewing and Predicting, Understanding Word Parts: the Prefixes *multi-* and *bi-,* Understanding Word Parts: The Suffixes *-ship* and *-ness*

Vocabulary:

animated	craze	heroine	spin-off
big hit	critiques	interfere	swap
brought a halt to	diversity	links	themes
categories	documentary	pilot	transmitted
character	eliminating	prime time	trial and error
contestants	episode	remodeled	

Points to Ponder

Add these questions to Exercise B, page 105:

How popular is television in your native country?

About how many hours each day do children in your country spend watching TV?

Chapter 1: The Early Days and Beyond (pages 106–113)

Reading

This selection offers a history of television as it has developed and improved, particularly during the twentieth century.

SKILL FOR SUCCESS: Using Graphic Organizers: Making a Timeline

Point out to students that making a timeline is another way to illustrate ideas, just as is making a chart, the graphic organizer they worked with in Unit 4. Timelines are useful because they help us to understand the sequence in which important events occurred.

EXTRA PRACTICE:

- Have students work individually to create a timeline of significant events in their lives.
- Have them begin with the date and place of birth and end with a significant and recent event that has occurred within the last three months.
- After timelines are completed, have students work in small groups, share their timelines, and talk about the events they included.
- You can also have the students put the timelines on poster board and hang them around the room.

SKILL FOR SUCCESS: Learning Homonyms

Point to students that because homonyms are spelled and often pronounced in the same way, using the context to help determine meaning is important. You can refer them to Unit 4, Skill for Success: Using Context Clues, page 98.

EXTRA PRACTICE: Have students write the meaning and part of speech for each of the underlined words from previous units. They can work individually, in pairs, or in small groups.

1. That ID card is fake.
2. The children fake being ill so they don't have to go to school.
3. Many celebrities contribute money to their favorite causes.
4. A jet airplane causes noise.
5. Radio stations often praise certain musicians.
6. The musician was inspired by the audience's praise.
7. Alternative fuels are becoming popular.
8. A difference of opinion often fuels an argument.
9. We gave the waiter a big tip because the service was great.
10. Please don't tip the glass. It's full and the water will spill.

Chapter 2: Dora the Explorer Leads the Way (pages 115–121)

Before You Read

Add these questions to Exercise A, page 115:

> What shows are there in your native country that are about a different culture or population? Do (or did) you watch them? Why or why not?

Reading

In this selection, students learn about how Dora, a Latino cartoon character, has been an important contribution to the development of TV shows about and for the Latino community.

After You Read

After students have completed the Comprehension Check on page 118, ask them to look back at the predictions they made in Exercise C, Previewing and Predicting, on page 115. Have them work in pairs to share their predictions and whether or not they were correct. Have students share specific information that helped them make accurate predictions.

FYI: *Dora the Explorer* has generated over $3 billion in retail sales of associated products since 2000, including $1 billion in 2004 alone.

SKILL FOR SUCCESS: Understanding Word Parts: The Prefixes *multi-* and *bi-*

Although the prefix *bi-* is often used with the words weekly and monthly, *biweekly* does not mean twice a week. It means every other week. Likewise, *bimonthly* means every other month, not twice a month. Knowing this distinction is especially important with respect to paychecks and payroll. Receiving a biweekly paycheck means a paycheck every two weeks.

Talk it Over

Add this question to the discussion questions on page 121:

> What shows do your children, or children you know, watch on TV? What do they like about these programs?

Chapter 3: Reality TV (pages 122–127)

Before You Read

Add this question to Exercise B, page 122:

> Why do you think reality TV has become popular?

Reading

In this reading, students are introduced to a relatively new concept in TV programming—Reality TV, or shows that present real people reacting in real situations.

SKILL FOR SUCCESS: Understanding Word Parts: The Suffixes *-ship* and *-ness*

EXTRA PRACTICE:

- Have students work in pairs to add *-ship* or *-ness* to the words below and write an original sentence for each new word. Have them use dictionaries to check spelling and meaning. Note: *hard* can be used with either suffix.

  citizen (*citizenship*)
  fair (*fairness*)
  happy (*happiness*)
  hard (*hardship; hardness*)
  homeless (*homelessness*)
  kin (*kinship*)
  nervous (*nervousness*)
  sad (*sadness*)
  scholar (*scholarship*)
  silly (*silliness*)

- Have pairs share their sentences with another pair.
- Have each pair put one or two sentences on the board.
- Review sentences as a class. Correct as necessary.

FYI: There are a number of precedents for reality TV, starting as far back as the 1940s in the United States. Allen Funt's television show *Candid Camera,* which began in 1948, filmed ordinary people in unusual situations, sometimes involving trick props, such as a desk with drawers that pop open when one is closed or a car with a hidden extra gas tank. Hidden cameras recorded the people's reactions.

Unit 5: Tie It All Together

Just for Fun

Bring in a video or DVD of a *Candid Camera* show and watch it as a class. Have the class discuss what was the funniest and why.

UNIT 6 SUPERSTITIONS

Theme: In Unit 6, students read about many kinds of superstitions.

Readings: The reading selections in this unit include a discussion of common superstitions about numbers, a highlight of some famous athletes and their superstitions, and some well-known things and places that people believe bring bad luck to their owners.

Skills for Success: Using Background Knowledge, Making Inferences, Scanning, Learning Homonyms, Using Graphic Organizers: Making a Chart, Skimming for the Main Idea, Identifying Facts and Opinions, Learning Synonyms and Antonyms, Using Background Information, Summarizing, Using Context Clues

Vocabulary:

acquire	hung up on	quirk	stick to
banned	illusion	rearranging	tragedies
blamed	legend	reputation	weird
eager	misfortune	rituals	
feast	notion	security	
hoaxes	passed up	skip	

Points to Ponder

Ask students to share some superstitions that are popular in their countries and if they personally believe them or not.

Chapter 1: It's Your Lucky Number! (pages 134–140)

Reading

All over the world, people have superstitions about certain numbers. In this selection, students learn about some superstitions associated with the number 13, as well as superstitions about a few other numbers.

After You Read

After students complete exercise A on page 136, have them share their answers from Exercise B on page 134 with a partner. Have partners talk about what they learned from the reading and whether or not they found that their answers in Exercise B were accurate.

SKILL FOR SUCCESS: Making Inferences

EXTRA PRACTICE: Have students work in small groups and discuss the following questions: Do you think the writer of this reading selection is superstitious? Why or why not?

SKILL FOR SUCCESS: Scanning

Review with the class the distinction between scanning for specific information and skimming for main ideas. Emphasize that both skills require reading quickly, but that the **focus** or **purpose** is different. When scanning, a reader looks for specific information or details. When skimming, the reader is trying to get a sense of what the entire article (or paragraph) is about—the big picture.

SKILL FOR SUCCESS: Learning Homonyms

Remind students that using context clues is an important skill to use when learning homonyms. It is often impossible to know the specific meaning of words in isolation. We usually look at an entire phrase or sentence to decide the meaning of the word. Knowing how a word functions in the sentence, i.e, its part of speech, is one clue that can give us an understanding of meaning.

SKILL FOR SUCCESS: Using Graphic Organizers: Making a Chart

EXTRA PRACTICE: Have students work in small groups or pairs to develop a chart based on the reading selection on pages 135–136. Before they begin, brainstorm some possible headings for the columns of the chart. Then talk about which headings would be appropriate to use and why or why not.

Chapter 2: Superstitious Athletes (pages 141–147)

Reading

This selection describes superstitions of several well-known athletes.

SKILL FOR SUCCESS: Learning Synonyms and Antonyms

After students have completed Exercise C on page 146, have them work in pairs to compare their answers. Then ask the class to explain how they decided on the answers. Did they guess? Did they know or recognize the words in each pair? Did they go back to the reading and use the context to decide on their answers?

EXTRA PRACTICE:

- Have students complete the following exercise without using dictionaries or other assistance.
- For each pair of words, have students circle *synonym* if the words are synonyms or *antonym* if the words are antonyms.

1. acquire	lose	synonym	antonym
2. banned	permitted	synonym	antonym
3. feast	banquet	synonym	antonym
4. notion	idea	synonym	antonym
5. rearranging	changing	synonym	antonym
6. security	safety	synonym	antonym
7. skip	include	synonym	antonym

- Have students work in pairs to compare their answers.
- Review the exercise as a class, but do not confirm whether or not answers are correct. Make a note on the board of items where there is disagreement about the correct answer.
- Have students scan the reading from Chapter 1 on pages 135–136 for the words in the first column of the chart and use context clues to decide on correct answers.
- Review each item from the exercise again, this time confirming correct answers.

Do Some Research

Have students use Google, Yahoo, or another Internet search engine to research specific holidays that are associated with superstitions. Have students prepare a short presentation about the holiday and its associated superstition(s) to share with the class.

Chapter 3: It's Jinxed! (pages 148–153)

Before You Read

- Before students begin Exercise A on page 148, ask them what they think the word *jinxed* means. Record their ideas on the board. Then have someone look up the definition for the word and read it aloud to the class. Put a check mark on the board next to any definitions that were accurate.
- Ask students to predict, based on the title, what the reading will be about. Make a note of their predictions on the board, and refer to them later after students have read the selection.

Reading

This selection is about the Hope Diamond and an ancient Egyptian tomb, both said to bring bad luck to those associated with them.

After You Read

FYI: Other common superstitions that are believed to bring bad luck:

- breaking a mirror
- walking under a ladder
- opening an umbrella inside the house
- entering a house left leg first
- using a red lighter

SKILL FOR SUCCESS: Summarizing

Point out to students that summarizing is a skill that they use regularly. It is simply expressing the main idea of something in your own words. Ask students to share situations in which they might summarize something (*telling a friend about a movie or a book, talking to family or friends about something that happened*).

EXTRA PRACTICE:

- Divide students into pairs or small groups and assign each pair or group one paragraph from either of the readings from Chapters 1 or 2 of this unit.

- Have each group write a summary of the paragraph on a piece of paper.
- When each pair or group has finished, have them read their summary and hang it at the front of the room.
- Have each pair or group use the paragraph summaries to write a short summary of the entire reading.

Unit 6: Tie It All Together

Video Activity: *The Pharaoh's* Curse

For Further Discussion

After students have completed Exercise C on page 155 of the Student Book, have them work in small groups to discuss the following:

> There are many famous legends—stories that are told from generation to generation that many people believe are true. Think about a famous legend that you know and share it with your group. Do you think it is true? Why or why not?

UNIT 7 OUR FRAGILE PLANET

Theme: In Unit 7, students learn about the delicate relationship between the earth and the people who inhabit it.

Readings: The reading selections in this unit present the Native American view about man's relationship to the land; endangered animal species, and some ways that people contribute to their extinction; and the threat and dangers of global warming.

Skills for Success: Using Background Knowledge, Making Inferences, Learning Homonyms, Previewing and Predicting, Understanding Cause and Effect, Understanding Word Parts: The Prefix *micro-*, Summarizing, Reading with a Purpose; Understanding Chain Reactions, Learning Synonyms and Antonyms, Using *Therefore* and *Because*

Vocabulary:

accelerating	countless	microscopic	tragic
chain reaction	fancy	pledge	treaty
conquest	grave	ramifications	vanished
conscious	habitats	sacred	vital
conservation	horrify	species	wildlife
convinced	intensifying	stick up for	

Points to Ponder

Before students begin discussing the questions on page 159, ask if they have heard of Earth Day and what they know about it. If no one knows anything about it, ask them to guess what they think Earth Day might be based on the title of this unit and the illustration on page 159.

Chapter 1: One Family with the Earth (pages 160–167)

Before You Read

Ask students what they know about Native Americans from the United States. Have students share what they know about the indigenous people in their own countries or indigenous people they know about in other countries.

FYI: There are about 150 Native American languages in Canada and the United States and another 600–700 languages in Central and South America.

Reading

This selection features an interview with Manitonquat, a Native American member of the Wampanoag Nation of Massachusetts, which highlights the Native American perspective on the earth and the relationship between the earth and its people.

SKILL FOR SUCCESS: Making Inferences

After students have completed the Comprehension Check on page 163, have them work in small groups to compare and discuss their answers.

For Further Research and Discussion

1. Have students use Google, Yahoo, or another Internet search engine to research and report on a group of indigenous people of their choice. The report can be oral, written, or both. Have students include information such as the name of the group or tribe, where they live, some of their common beliefs and practices, and how the group lives in the twenty-first century.
2. Read Shel Silverstein's *The Giving Tree* to the class. Have students work in small groups to write a summary of the story. Use the summaries as a basis for discussion about the message of this story.

Chapter 2: Our Endangered Wildlife (pages 168–174)

Reading

The reading highlights a few of the earth's endangered species and a brief discussion of how people threaten the survival of various animals in the world.

SKILL FOR SUCCESS: Understanding Cause and Effect

- Point out to students that their study of superstitions in Unit 6 is a great example of cause and effect. Superstitions, however, are based on **irrational** beliefs that a certain event in the present will cause a future effect. For hundreds of years, scientists have studied cause and effect in an effort to rationally explain **why** certain things occur in the world.
- After students have completed Exercise B on pages 171–172, have them work in small groups to discuss a scientific or medical discovery that has changed the way we think about certain things. For example, in the twenty-first century, there is scientific proof that

smoking causes cancer, premature birth, and low birth weights in newborn children. Have each group share their ideas with the class.

EXTRA PRACTICE: Have students reread the interview in Chapter 1 on pages 161–162. Have them work in pairs to make a chart of causes and effects that Manitonquat discusses in the interview and to share their charts with the class. Hang the charts around the room.

SKILL FOR SUCCESS: Understanding Word Parts: The Prefix *micro-*

As they write definitions for the words in Exercise C on page 173, ask students to note the part of speech for each word as well. Point out that each of these words is a noun except for *microwave,* which can also be a verb. After they have completed Exercise D on page 173, have them work in pairs to write an original sentence for each of the words from Exercise C. Ask six pairs to write one of their sentences on the board. Review with the class and correct as necessary, paying particular attention to errors in usage, e.g., a noun used as an adjective.

Make a Poster

To support this activity, have students visit www.endangeredspecie.com to find information and ideas for the posters. Hang the posters around the room.

Chapter 3: The Heat Is On! (pages 175–181)

Reading

This selection is about a few of the causes and effects of global warming.

SKILL FOR SUCCESS: Understanding Chain Reactions

- Have students share as a class what cause-and-effect signal words they found and underlined as they read "The Heat Is On!" Write them on the board.
- Then have students complete the chart in Exercise B.

SKILL FOR SUCCESS: Summarizing

EXTRA PRACTICE: After students have completed Exercise C on page 179, have them share their summaries in pairs or small groups. Then have each group write a group summary based on their individual summaries and make a chart on poster board that graphically represents their summary of the article.

SKILL FOR SUCCESS: Using *Therefore* and *Because*

EXTRA PRACTICE: Have students select information from one of the cause-and-effect charts they made for the Extra Practice in Chapter 2 and write two sentences about each cause and effect. In one sentence they should use *therefore* and in the other *because.* Select various students to write sentences on the board. Review and correct as necessary.

For Further Study

Have students watch and discuss *An Inconvenient Truth,* a movie about global warming featuring Al Gore.

Unit 7: Tie It All Together

Video Activity: *The Eagles Return*

Add these questions to Exercise C on page 183 of the Student Book:

> Are there any endangered species in your home country? What are they? What are people doing to help this endangered species recover? Do you think they will be successful? Why or why not?

Just for Fun

Create your own Earth Day Celebration. Declare a day as Earth Day in your school. Invite some other classes to share in your celebration. Have students share their thoughts about Earth Day and what it means to them. Ask them to display and do a short presentation about the Earth Day Stamp they designed. They could also share a favorite story or legend about an animal with the group. Then serve some light refreshments—but paper cups and paper plates only, please!

UNIT 8 LIVING A LONG LIFE

Theme: In Unit 8, students take a look at some research about the process of aging and some elderly citizens who have accomplished astonishing things in their older years.

Readings: The first reading selection features explorer and adventurer Dan Buetter and his unusual inquiry into the aging population of Okinawa, Japan, where people live on average seven years longer than the average American. The second selection is the story of the famous athlete Joe Lewis and lessons he learned about life from his father. The final reading focuses on research about aging and the effects of diet and exercise on the human brain.

Skills for Success: Using Background Knowledge, Making Inferences, Understanding Word Parts: Root Words; the Suffix *-ology,* Identifying Facts and Opinions, Learning Idioms: Parts of the Body, Learning Three-Word Verbs

Vocabulary:

come up with	extraordinarily	peaked	rich
common sense	fatigue	pioneer	toddlers
competent	feats	plain	turns it on its head
concentrate	foremost	principle	
confidence	give up	quest	
endurance	hung out with	regardless	

Points to Ponder

Add these questions to the discussion questions on page 187:

> How do you imagine yourself living near the end of your life? Where will you be? What will you be doing?

Chapter 1: Discovering the Secrets to a Long Life (pages 188—194)

Before You Read

FYI: One of the biggest jumps in life expectancy coincided with the introduction of sewers, which greatly reduced the spread of disease.

Reading

This selection highlights an inquiry into the aging population of Okinawa, Japan, through the use of an interactive expedition, which allowed explorers at home to "accompany" and direct an on-site exploration team in Okinawa.

After You Read

You and your students can visit the Blue Zones website at www.bluezones.com, where you will find information about the Okinawa expedition as well as information about upcoming expeditions that you can join.

SKILL FOR SUCCESS: Understanding Word Parts: Root Words; the Suffix *-ology*

Point out to students that not all words ending in *-ology* mean *the study of.* In some words such as *haplology,* the *-ology* suffix is from the Greek *logos,* meaning *word,* and indicates not a field of study but a type of speech or writing. For example, *haplology* means the mistake of saying one letter, syllable, or word when two or more are required, as in the example of pronouncing the word *February* somewhat like *Febuary.*
Also point out that some words mean *the study of* but don't end in *-ology,* such as *midwifery,* which can mean the practice of helping women deliver babies or the study of this practice.

EXTRA PRACTICE: Have students complete the chart below and then use each new word in an original sentence.

Field of Study	Job	Meaning
audiology		
	bacteriologist	
	criminologist	
ecology		
geology		
	graphologist	

Chapter 2: What Makes a Champion (pages 195-200)

Before You Read

FYI: Joe Lewis is a world famous American martial artist and then karate master. He is not the same person as Joe Louis, a great American boxing champion.

Reading

In this selection, athlete Joe Lewis tells about some important lessons he learned about life from his father.

SKILL FOR SUCCESS: Learning Idioms: Parts of the Body

Remind students that idioms have a meaning different from the meanings of the individual words. Idioms with parts of the body are quite common.

EXTRA PRACTICE: Have students use Google, Yahoo, or another Internet search engine for *idioms, parts of the body*. They will find several interactive websites that feature various games and activities relating to these idioms. Have each student find two more idioms that refer to parts of the body and share them with the class.

Chapter 3: Good News for the Aging Brain (pages 201–205)

Reading

In this article, students learn about the aging human brain and things we can do to keep our minds active as we grow older.

Read a Graph

- Point out to students that the graphs on page 205 are bar graphs, a type of graphic organizer that is often used to present data.
- Before they begin the exercise, look at the graphs together as a class and support students in clarifying the information that is presented in each bar graph and how the information in each individual graph is related.
- For example, in the top graph, the vertical axis represents the number of people (in millions), while the vertical axis on the bottom graph represents the percentage of the population.
- Both graphs are referring to the segment of the population that is over age 65.
- After students have completed the exercise, have them work in pairs to compare their answers. Then review the exercise together as a class.

Unit 8: Tie It All Together

Video Activity: *Longevity Gene*

Add these questions to Exercise C on page 207 of the Student Book:

> Do you know anyone who (has) lived to be 100 years old or more? What is (was) this person like?

Just for Fun

Have each student create a poster that represents what he or she wants life to be like in the older years. Students can cut out pictures from magazines and paste them on poster board or make original drawings. Ask students to include representations of the following in their posters:

- Where will they be living?
- Who are the specific people they will be with?
- What will they be doing?
- What will they want others to remember about them?

Display completed posters around the room and have each student share about his or her poster with the class.

UNIT TESTS AND ANSWER KEY

NAME

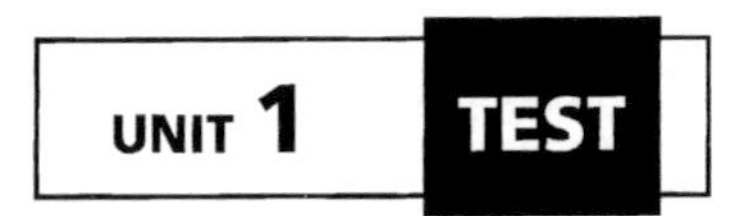

Read the article.

Cross-Cultural Disconnections

There is often great misunderstanding associated with tourists and business people who go to other countries, because customs vary greatly among cultures. In some cultures a certain gesture or action signifies something polite and respectful, while in others the same gesture is considered rude and disrespectful. Language often changes meaning when it is translated; people think they are saying one thing but are really saying something else.

Big companies do extensive research before sending their products to other countries. Yet there are many stories of businesses that sometimes find themselves in complicated situations because they do not understand customs in foreign cultures. Take, for example, the executives who thought they had the perfect advertisement for their cologne for men: a picture of a man and his dog. Unfortunately, in North Africa, where the cologne was sold, a dog is considered unclean and a sign of bad luck. In another story, executives at General Motors thought their economical car, the Chevy Nova, was a logical choice for people in Latin America. However, the little car did not sell. They realized too late that in Spanish, *no va* means "it doesn't go." Once, a well-known shoe company made a television ad to sell its sports shoes. The ad showed people from different countries saying, "Just do it!" in their native language. Later the company found out that a Samburu African tribesman was really saying, "I don't want these, give me big shoes." For years, Gerber sold its famous baby food with the picture of a baby on the label. They did not know that in one particular country the picture on the label represents the food inside the jar!

Tourists also deal with unexpected events and problems because of cultural misunderstandings. One American couple was traveling with their pet dog in an Asian country. At a restaurant, they tried to tell the waiter that their dog was also hungry. At first, they were pleased when the waiter took the dog to the kitchen. They thought the dog would get some food. They were horrified when the waiter returned later with the cooked dog! Once a young woman was visiting with her boyfriend's family in Spain. She was telling the family a story about something embarrassing that had happened to her. She said that she was "muy embarazada," which, in Spanish, means "very pregnant." Her boyfriend's parents became quite upset, and the girl was extremely embarrassed—again!

Although customs are passed down from generation to generation in countries all over the world, they are often terribly misunderstood when people try to pass them from one country to another. Perhaps the best advice for international businesses and travelers is expressed in this simple saying: When in Rome, do as the Romans do. And, of course, before going anywhere, be a considerate and responsible traveler and learn as much about the culture as possible to avoid a complete cultural disconnection.

Part 1 *(10 points)*

A. ***Circle the correct answer to complete each main idea.***

1. Paragraph 1

Cultural differences ______.

a. are often seen in gestures or actions

b. often create serious misunderstanding

c. happen through language translations

2. Paragraph 2

Businesses selling their products in foreign countries ______.

a. lose business when they don't understand the culture

b. lose business because of poor advertising

c. need to have better translators

3. Paragraph 3

Tourists who travel to other countries ______.

a. have trouble communicating in restaurants

b. often misunderstand the language

c. have some upsetting surprises

4. Paragraph 4

Customs ______.

a. are generally passed down through generations

b. are often misunderstood from one culture to another

c. should be honored by tourists and business people

B. ***Read these statements. If the statement is true, write* T *on the line. If it is false, write* F.**

_____ **1.** Meanings of gestures and actions often vary among countries.

_____ **2.** One car manufacturer couldn't sell a certain car because of its name.

_____ **3.** The sports shoe ad was very successful.

_____ **4.** A waiter brought food for a tourist couple's dog.

_____ **5.** One woman's poor communication created a misunderstanding with her boyfriend's family.

_____ **6.** In order to avoid problems, it is important to know something about a foreign culture.

Part 2 *(20 points)*

A. ***Complete the chart. Add the prefix* il-, ir-, im-, *or* in-.**

considerate	
logical	
perfect	
polite	
responsible	

Now, fill in the blanks with the words from the completed chart.

1. The cologne company's ad was ______________.

2. Tourists often appear ______________ because they don't understand the culture.

3. Some businesses are ______________ about their advertising in foreign countries.

4. The Chevy Nova was an ______________ choice for Latin America.

5. Certain gestures are seen as ______________ in some countries.

B. *Complete the chart. Add* **-tion** *to each verb to make a noun.*

realize	
generate	
situate	
disconnect	
consider	

Now, fill in the blanks with the words from the completed chart.

1. Each new ______________ in a culture learns customs from the previous one.

2. Big companies should have ______________ of language, customs, and cultures when they advertise in foreign countries.

3. Misunderstandings about customs in other countries can create cultural ______________.

4. The young woman who said she was "very pregnant" was in an uncomfortable ______________.

5. Sometimes businesses come to the ______________ too late that they have misunderstood a foreign culture.

NAME

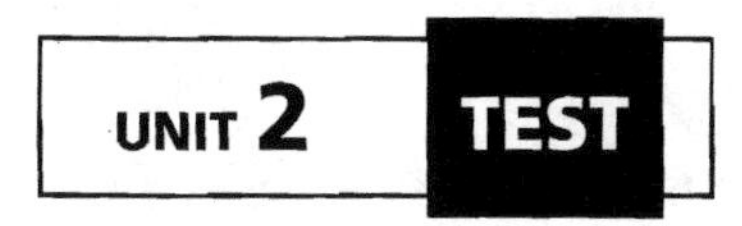

Read the article.

The Magnificent Mount Rushmore

Mount Rushmore National Memorial, near Keystone, South Dakota, is a United States Presidential Memorial that represents the first 150 years of the history of the United States of America. In a few thousand years, our descendants may look at this magnificent monument and wonder how human beings in the twentieth century created it. The sixty-foot sculptures* of former U.S. Presidents George Washington, Thomas Jefferson, Theodore Roosevelt, and Abraham Lincoln may one day fascinate the people of the future, just as the Easter Island Statues or the Nazca Lines intrigue us.

The project of carving Mount Rushmore originally began as a way to increase tourism in the Black Hills of South Dakota. Doane Robinson, a historian, thought of the idea and brought artist Gutzon Borglum to the Black Hills to look at the mountains. Originally, Borglum was going to carve the monument in some stone pillars called the Needles. However, he realized that that plan could not be carried out because the Needles were too thin to support the sculpture. He chose Mount Rushmore, a better spot, because it faced southeast and had maximum exposure to the sun. Borglum speculated that the project would take six years and cost about $500,000. He would be shocked to learn that it took 14 years to complete at a cost of nearly $1 million, which came mostly from the federal government.

Between October 4, 1927 and October 31, 1941, Gutzon Borglum cooperated with nearly 400 workers to carve the faces of Presidents George Washington, Thomas Jefferson, Theodore Roosevelt, and Abraham Lincoln. Each head is 60 feet high, or 80 times the size of the average human head. George Washington's nose is 20 feet long, and each of his eyes is 11 feet wide. The width of Thomas Jefferson's mouth is 18 feet. An estimated 450,000 tons of rock was removed. Some of the men's tools weighed as much as 85 pounds. No one died as they worked more than a mile above sea level on the face of the mountain, but there is evidence that several workers died later from lung problems caused by breathing the granite powder in the air. By July 4, 1934, Washington's face was completed and was dedicated. The face of Thomas Jefferson was dedicated in 1936, and the face of Abraham Lincoln was dedicated on September 17, 1937. In 1939, the face of Theodore Roosevelt was dedicated. However, the final dedication did not take place until July 3, 1991, when President George H.W. Bush visited the mountain.

Mount Rushmore sparked controversy among Native Americans because the United States took the area from the Lakota tribe after the Black Hills War in 1876–77. The Lakota consider the hills to be sacred, but some historians believe the Lakota took control of the hills from the Cheyenne in 1776 with weapons and violence. In response to the sensation among Native Americans caused by Mount Rushmore, the Crazy Horse Memorial is being built elsewhere in the Black Hills to honor a famous Indian leader. It is intended to be larger than Mount Rushmore and has the support of Lakota chiefs. However, it is not financed with federal funds.

*sculpture = a statue often carved from stone

Part 1 *(12 points)*

A. ***Read these statements. If the statement is true, write* T *on the line. If it is false, write* F.**

_____ **1.** Mount Rushmore was created several hundred years ago.

_____ **2.** There are 60 different sculptures at Mount Rushmore.

_____ **3.** It took nearly six years to complete Mount Rushmore.

_____ **4.** The first face completed and dedicated was George Washington's.

_____ **5.** This famous memorial is appreciated and honored by all Americans.

_____ **6.** The Crazy Horse Memorial was built before Mount Rushmore.

B. ***Scan the article to match each item on the left with the correct item on the right. Write the letter of the correct answer on the line.***

1. _____ 14 years a. the final cost of Mount Rushmore

2. _____ 60 feet b. the year of the final dedication

3. _____ nearly $1million c. the size of George Washington's nose

4. _____1991 d. time it took to complete Mount Rushmore

5. _____ 20 feet e. the years of the Black Hills War

6. _____ 1876–77 f. the size of each president's head

Part 2 *(13 points)*

A. ***Write the letter of the word or phrase in the box that means the same as the underlined word.***

a. guessed	b. caused	c. impressive	d. proof	e. cut	f. surprised

_____ **1.** . . . our descendants may look at this <u>magnificent</u> memorial . . .

_____ **2.** Originally, Borglum was going to <u>carve</u> the monument . . .

_____ **3.** Borglum <u>speculated</u> that the project would take six years . . .

_____ **4.** He would be <u>shocked</u> to learn that it took 14 years . . .

_____ **5.** . . . but there is <u>evidence</u> that several workers died from lung problems . . .

_____ **6.** Mount Rushmore <u>sparked</u> controversy among Native Americans . . .

B. ***Write the letter of the correct answer on the line.***

1. _____ biologist a. someone who studies events of the past

2. _____ cooperate b. live with

3. _____ coauthor c. someone who can help you find a book

4. _____ historian d. a person who studies numbers

5. _____ librarian e. work with

6. _____ statistician f. a person who writes a book together with another person.

7. _____ coexist g. a person who studies plants and animals

NAME

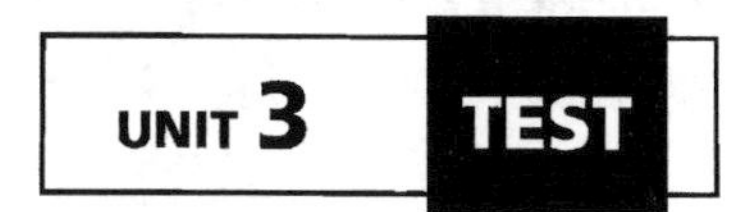

Read the article.

A Good Jingle Sells It All

A jingle is a short song that includes a phrase people can easily remember. It is used in advertisements for a product that a company wants to sell. Jingles became very popular in the United States during the 1950s. They were written to advertise breakfast cereals, candy, snacks, hamburgers, hot dogs, and many other products that the public purchases. A good jingle is written so that it remains in the listener's memory long after it is first heard. People often remember a jingle for years after the product it advertised is gone, and you may remember some of these. Are you hungry? "You deserve a break today!" Are you looking for a delicious hamburger? "Have it your way." Do you want a bowl of delicious soup? Try one that's "M'm! M'm! Good!"

JAM Creative Productions in Dallas, Texas, wrote many of the most memorable jingles. The company, founded in 1974 by Jonathan and Mary Lyn Wolfert, makes more radio jingles than any other company and has become a part of American popular culture. It is the only company of its type that has been continuously owned and operated by its founders for more than 30 years. JAM also produces jingles for celebrity clients, such as well-known TV and radio stations and their famous announcers. One of JAM's largest clients is the BBC (British Broadcasting Corporation).

Jonathan Wolfert became interested in jingles while growing up in New York City. He loved listening to the radio and wondered who wrote the short little songs that announced the radio station. He thought that work at a jingle company would allow him to combine his musical, audio production, and radio skills. He began work at PAMS, a jingle producer in Dallas. After three years, he started his own company, and JAM was officially born in 1974. He began in the extra bedroom of his home and rented time in a studio when needed. By 1977, JAM bought and renovated the studio it was renting. By 1987, JAM was so popular that it needed a second studio, so a new 14,000 square foot building was constructed.

So what's new for JAM and the jingle business? It's the Personal Cut, a jingle designed for individuals. If you want to create a lively holiday greeting for your family and friends, a composer at JAM will be delighted to make it for you. If you would like a calming music CD when you find the world annoying, JAM will put it together. And if you need inspirational music, JAM has it. You can order something to kick off an event or deliver an essential message. Whether you're world-famous, a radio station, a super star, or an ordinary person, JAM is committed to delivering a new, interesting, and effective way to sell through high-quality music and production. As Jonathan Wolfert says, "It's a lot of work, but it's better than having a real job."

Part 1 *(14 points)*

A. *Read these statements. If a statement is true, write* **T** *on the line. If it is false, write* **F.**

_____ **1.** A jingle consists of words and music.

_____ **2.** Jingles advertise only food products.

_____ **3.** JAM is a rock band.

_____ **4.** Jonathan Wolfert created PAMS.

_____ **5.** JAM produces jingles for business and individual clients.

B. *Read these statements. If the statement is a fact, write* **F** *on the line. If it is an opinion, write* **O.**

_____ **1.** Jingles are a great way to sell products.

_____ **2.** Jonathan Wolfert loved listening to the radio.

_____ **3.** JAM was founded in 1974.

_____ **4.** The Personal Cut is a clever way to connect with family and friends.

_____ **5.** By 1987, JAM needed a second studio.

C. *Circle the letter of the statement that best expresses the main idea of the paragraph.*

1. Paragraph 1

a. Jingles are short phrases with music.

b. A good jingle and the product it advertises are remembered for a long time.

c. "Have it your way," is an example of a jingle.

2. Paragraph 2

a. JAM is a well-known and well-respected company.

b. JAM has been owned and operated by the same people for 30 years.

c. The BBC is a client of JAM.

3. Paragraph 3

a. Jonathan Wolfert loved the radio.

b. Wolfert worked at PAMS before starting JAM.

c. JAM started as a small company and grew very quickly.

4. Paragraph 4

a. The Personal Cut is a new kind of jingle.

b. JAM has expanded its market by selling to individuals as well as businesses.

c. Being the owner of JAM is a lot of work.

Part 2 *(11 points)*

A. ***Circle the letter of the word or phrase that has the same meaning as the boldface word in the sentence.***

1. One of JAM's **clients** is the BBC.

a. victims   b. customers

2. A composer at JAM will be **delighted** to make it.

a. very happy   b. bright

3. Would you like calming music when you find the world **annoying?**

a. noisy   b. irritating

4. You can order something to **kick off** an event.

a. start   b. injure

5. JAM is **committed** to delivering a new, interesting, and effective way to sell.

a. dedicated   b. promising

B. ***Circle the word in each group that does not belong.***

1. lively	slow	active	energetic
2. essential	necessary	basic	extra
3. calming	relaxing	irritating	soothing
4. inspirational	moving	dull	sacred
5. praise	congratulate	approve of	criticize
6. celebrity	unknown	famous	recognized

NAME

Read the article.

It's All in a Day's Play

The twenty-first–century focus on alternative, renewable energy has sparked an interest in an unusual product made in South Africa: the Roundabout PlayPump. It uses the energy of children at play to operate a water pump and is made by the South African company Roundabout Outdoor. At present, nearly 700 PlayPumps in Africa provide clean drinking water to more than 1 million people. If the idea catches on, there could be 4,000 pumps operating in the next ten years, providing water to more than 10 million people in Africa.

The PlayPump is a simple and practical solution to a major problem in many places in the world: a lack of clean drinking water. Especially in Asia and Africa, there are small villages that have no water systems. Women and children spend up to six hours a day carrying water from rivers that are often very far away. PlayPumps allow children to spend time in school instead of carrying water and enables women to spend time at home or doing other things that provide additional food or income to their families. The PlayPump also provides the children with exercise and an opportunity to convert ordinary play into something that benefits the whole community.

The PlayPump is like a playground merry-go-round attached to a water pump. The merry-go-round is a large round tube with bars. The children hold on to the handles and run along the outside of the round tube. When the circular tube is going fast enough, the children jump on and ride until it stops spinning. This spinning motion pumps underground water into a large tank above the ground. Two of the four sides of the storage tank are used to advertise products, and the other two sides are devoted to public health messages. The pump can raise up to 370 gallons (about 1,400 liters) of water per hour from a depth of up to 328 feet (100 meters). Extra water goes back into the ground. The pumps require an initial investment of about $9,000, and the advertising boards above the pump raise the funds for maintenance.

The PlayPump is proof that creative solutions can be used to overcome what seem like impossible problems in today's world. Roundabout Outdoor has created a partnership with the South African Department of Water Affairs and Forestry to help meet commitments to supply water to rural communities. Nonprofit organizations are working to entice companies and individuals to invest in this promising answer to a worldwide problem. They are hoping that by word of mouth and Internet advertising, the PlayPump will sell like hotcakes. Who knows? By the middle of this century maybe no one will ever run out of water again.

Who would ever have imagined that "child power" would be used as a renewable energy source? It may just be a fad, but recently the PlayPump won the World Bank's Development Marketplace Award for its effectiveness both at pumping water and communicating public health messages.

Part 1 *(15 points)*

A. ***Read these statements. If the statement is a fact, write* F *on the line. If it is an opinion, write* O.**

_____ **1.** More than 1 million people get their water from PlayPumps.

_____ **2.** The pumps cost $9,000 to buy.

_____ **3.** PlayPump is a creative solution to a big problem in the world.

_____ **4.** Roundabout Outdoor and the South African government have a partnership.

_____ **5.** "Child power" is a great renewable energy source.

_____ **6.** The PlayPump is a highly effective way to get water.

B. ***Write* M *if the statement expresses the main idea of the paragraph. Write* I *if the statement gives supporting information.***

1. Paragraph 1

_____ a. The PlayPump uses the energy of children to operate a water pump.

_____ b. The Roundabout PlayPump is an unusual new product from South Africa.

_____ c. Nearly 700 PlayPumps in Africa provide clean drinking water to more than one million people.

2. Paragraph 2

_____ a. Women and children spend up to six hours a day carrying water.

_____ b. PlayPumps allow children to spend more time in school.

_____ c. The PlayPump is a simple and practical solution to a major problem.

3. Paragraph 3

_____ a. The PlayPump is like a merry-go-round attached to a water pump.

_____ b. The merry-go-round is a large round tube with bars.

_____ c. The pump can raise up to 370 gallons (1,400 liters) of water per hour.

Part 2 *(10 points)*

A. ***Circle the letter of the word or phrase that has the same meaning as the* boldface *word in the sentence.***

1. If the idea **catches on,** there could be 4,000 pumps operating in the next ten years.

a. volunteers b. becomes popular

2. The twenty-first–century focus on **alternative**, renewable energy has sparked an interest in an unusual product.

a. another b. changed

3. The PlayPump provides an opportunity to **convert** ordinary play into something that benefits the whole community.

a. take b. change

4. Nonprofit organizations are working to **entice** companies and individuals to invest.

a. persuade b. charge

5. Nonprofit organizations are working to entice companies and individuals to **invest.**

a. spend money b. attract

B. *Answer each question with* **Yes** *or* **No.**

1. If a solution is practical, is it sensible? ______

2. Does proof show that something is true? ______

3. Would the ocean run out of water? ______

4. Is word of mouth a way to advertise? ______

5. If products sell like hotcakes, do they sell slowly? ______

NAME

Read the article.

The Great American Quiz Show Scam*

One popular type of television program in the 1950s was the quiz show. Contestants on the show were asked questions that required knowledge in many different categories. As contestants answered more difficult questions, they would win larger amounts of money. People often achieved huge financial success on these shows, and audiences loved to watch contestants become wealthy by using their brain power.

One of the most famous was the prime-time TV show *Twenty One.* Two contestants, a champion and a challenger, stood in separate booths. They could not see or hear each other. Contestants answered questions and won points for correct answers. The more points a question was worth, the more difficult the question was. Each game ran for several rounds. If the champion won the game, he would win money and a new challenger would be called in. If the champion lost, he would be off the show and the winning challenger would become the new champion. A champion continued to play for as long as he continued to win the games. Audiences loved to watch the show, and it eventually became a big hit.

On November 28, 1956, Charles Van Doren, a college professor, appeared as a challenger to the champion, Herbert Stempel. The two men played for several weeks, but neither scored enough points to win the game. As each episode continued, the show became a popular craze. However, most viewers did not like Stempel. They preferred Van Doren, who appeared charming and genuine. After many weeks, Stempel gave an incorrect answer and lost the game. Once Van Doren became champion, he remained on the show for one of the longest time periods of any game show contestant. As a result of this success, he signed a contract for *The Today Show,* and even was on the cover of *Time* magazine.

Later, the scam was revealed to the public. People learned that in the beginning, *Twenty One* was not very popular and audiences were bored. The producers of the show began to tell the contestants how to dress and what to say. They also gave contestants answers to the questions and told them which questions to answer and which ones to miss. The charming Charles Van Doren admitted that he had been given questions and answers before the show and was deeply involved in the deception of millions of people.

Twenty One was suddenly cancelled in October 1958. The public no longer trusted this early form of reality TV, and the scam interfered with the success of everyone involved. Charles Van Doren resigned from his university teaching position and was dropped from *The Today Show*. Producer Dan Enright had to move to Canada to continue his career. The host and co-producer, Jack Barry, did not host another national TV show for nearly ten years. The success of the Great American Quiz Show was brought to a halt, nearly eliminating a type of show that for many Americans was the best of "reality TV."

*scam = a plan for making money illegally or dishonestly

Part 1 *(20 points)*

A. *Circle the correct answer.*

1. Contestants on the quiz shows of the 1950s ______.

a. asked difficult questions

b. often became financially successful

c. had to know a lot about one category

2. On *Twenty One,* there were ______.

a. several contestants playing the game together

b. two rounds in each game

c. champions who played for more than one episode

3. Charles Van Doren and Herb Stempel ______.

a. played the game for several weeks but neither won

b. were charming and very popular with audiences

c. college professors

4. The big scam was that ______.

a. in the beginning audiences were bored

b. producers gave contestants answers to the questions before the show

c. Charles Van Doren was not really a college professor

5. After the truth about *Twenty One* was revealed, ______.

a. the show became extremely popular

b. all quiz shows were immediately cancelled

c. people from the show faced big challenges in their lives

B. *Write the letter of the correct answer from the box on the line.*

a. Dan Enright	b. Herbert Stempel	c. *Time*	d. *The Today Show*	e. two

_____ **1.** A TV show on which Charles Van Doren appeared

_____ **2.** The producer who moved to Canada to continue his career

_____ **3.** A contestant on a famous quiz show of the 1950s

_____ **4.** A magazine that had Charles Van Doren on the cover

_____ **5.** The number of contestants who played the game on *Twenty One*

Part 2 *(5 points)*

Circle the word that doesn't belong.

1. ended	carried	stopped	brought to a halt
2. groups	categories	classes	animals
3. competitor	contestant	answer	challenger
4. trend	craze	fad	insane
5. came between	interfered	cooperated	interrupted

NAME

Read the article.

Superstitious Sports Say It's the Curse

It is common knowledge that sports fans and athletes are superstitious. It is no surprise, then, that there are superstitions about the misfortune of baseball teams in their attempts to win the biggest competition in the world of baseball: the World Series. The World Series occurs every October at the end of baseball season in the United States. Every year, two competitors—championship teams from the American and National baseball leagues—play up to seven games to determine which team in the United States is the best.

Two famous legends about baseball and the World Series are the Curse of the Black Sox and the Curse of the Bambino. Although each has a different story, both are the reason eager fans use to explain why their teams didn't win. Like other superstitions, these "curses" are based on a belief that future events are caused by specific behaviors.

In 1919, the American League's Chicago White Sox played against the National League's Cincinnati Reds. At that time, betting on sports events was popular. Professional gamblers enticed several players on the Chicago team to lose the World Series. The gamblers bet on Cincinnati and made a mint. In return, they promised to pay the Chicago players $100,000. However, the hoax was eventually revealed, and the team's reputation was ruined. Eight players were banned from baseball, and the shocked public called the team the Black Sox. Between 1919 and 1958, the Sox did not win another American League Championship. Why? People will say it was the Curse of the Black Sox. The "curse" continued, fans say, when the White Sox played in the 1959 World Series and lost. It was not until 2005, when they won a World Series after 86 years, that the Curse of the Black Sox ended.

By 1919, Babe Ruth was a star player on the Boston Red Sox, but the team's owner sold Babe Ruth to the New York Yankees in 1920. The fans thought this was one of the greatest tragedies of baseball. People say it was then that the Curse of the Bambino (Spanish for "baby") began for the Red Sox. Before Babe Ruth left the team, the Red Sox had won five of the first fifteen World Series. After he left, the Red Sox played in the Series four times and lost each time. In 2004, the Red Sox won the World Series and fans say the curse was broken. In the 84 years of the "curse," Red Sox fans tried various weird notions and rituals to break it. One group placed a Red Sox baseball cap on top of Mt. Everest, the highest mountain in the world. Another group hired priests to purify the baseball park.

Is it a quirk, an illusion, or something else? Some sports fans will stick to the story that their teams didn't acquire the championship because of the curses, but they can't explain what events suddenly eliminated those curses. Who knows? One day someone might develop a theory about that!

Part 1 *(15 points)*

A. ***Check the statements that are inferences based on the information in the article.***

_____ **1.** Baseball fans love the World Series.

_____ **2.** Some sports fans don't accept the notion that their teams lose because they don't play as well as the team that wins.

_____ **3.** In 1919, the Chicago White Sox played against the Cincinnati Reds.

_____ **4.** The owner of the Boston Red Sox sold a star player to another team.

_____ **5.** Red Sox fans were very serious about the Curse of the Bambino.

B. ***Write* O *for Opinion or* F *for Fact on the line before each statement.***

_____ **1.** Each year two teams play in the World Series.

_____ **2.** When a team loses the World Series, it is unfortunate.

_____ **3.** The gamblers promised to pay the Chicago players a lot of money.

_____ **4.** Selling Babe Ruth to the New York Yankees was a bad decision.

_____ **5.** Before Babe Ruth left the team, the Red Sox had won five World Series.

C. ***Write the correct answer on the line next to each phrase.***

1. The maximum number of games in the World Series _______________

2. The amount of money the White Sox players were promised _______________

3. The number of years it took the White Sox to win another World Series _______________

4. The year Babe Ruth left the Red Sox _______________

5. The number of years of the Curse of the Bambino _______________

Part 2 *(10 points)*

A. ***Cross out the word in each group that does not belong.***

1. legends	stories	facts	tales
2. eager	disinterested	excited	enthusiastic
3. permitted	allowed	accepted	banned
4. normal	usual	weird	regular
5. obtain	get	lose	acquire

B. ***Use context clues to write a definition or synonym for each underlined word.***

1. There are superstitions about the <u>misfortunes</u> of baseball teams.

2. The <u>hoax</u> was eventually revealed.

3. Red Sox fans tried various weird <u>notions</u> and rituals.

4. Is it a quirk, an <u>illusion</u>, or something in between?

5. Some sports fans <u>stick to</u> their stories about why their teams didn't win.

NAME

Read the article.

Methane Gas and Art: Now, That's Incredible!

Something unusual is happening in the mountains of North Carolina. Designers and engineers are working together to create the Craft Campus at University of North Carolina in Asheville. It will be an art building for students that provides studio space for work with clay, metal, wood, and glass. In addition to art studios, there will be classrooms, offices, an art gallery, and a visitors' center.

What's unusual about that? The building's primary energy source will be methane gas from a nearby landfill, a place where tons of garbage collected from area residents is dumped. Methane gas from the landfill will provide electricity for lights, hot water, and machines that run on electrical power. It will also run the huge furnaces and ovens that are required for art work made from clay and glass. Now, that's incredible!

The landfill, which closed down in 1998, is an unused energy source. It holds about 3,300,000 tons (6,600,000,000 pounds) of garbage. The methane gas produced from this garbage, converted to electricity, would be enough to provide power to approximately 2,000 homes. That's a lot of electricity, and conservation groups are convinced that the partnership between the university and Buncombe County is a vital contribution to saving the environment. The project will reduce the amount of gas released into the air. This is important because methane can be a grave danger. It is a greenhouse gas that contributes to accelerating global warming. As a result, using the landfill's methane gas for power reduces the danger and provides a stable, reliable source of energy.

The campus will be fully "green." This means that in addition to using landfill methane for its energy needs, builders will use recycled materials. Materials will be locally produced so that energy is saved in shipping, and they will be produced using low amounts of energy. Therefore, this new campus will show others how to use alternative energy and recycled materials.

The Craft Campus will also be designed to require less energy for climate control. For example, there will be windows that face the south with trees in front of them. Light and heat from the sun will come in through the leafless trees in winter, but in the summer the leaves on the trees will prevent the heat from intensifying and making the building too warm. Consequently, the building will need less electricity.

The project has other ramifications, too. The new campus will relieve crowding in the studios and classrooms in the present building. Every year the university turns away students because there isn't enough studio space. The project also comes at a particularly good time in western North Carolina, where art is now an important part of the economy. Years ago, the economy was based on manufacturing of furniture and fabrics, but many of those businesses have vanished. This partnership is the first of its kind in the world and is sure to be an example for countless people of how to make conscious decisions that will protect our fragile planet.

Part 1 *(15 points)*

A. *Complete the chart with statements from the box to show two chain reactions.*

gas is released into the atmosphere	electricity provides power for an art building	garbage is taken to a landfill	greenhouse effect becomes stronger	gas is converted to electricity
the earth gets warmer	plants and animals die	artists create things to show and sell	garbage produces methane gas	people make and spend more money

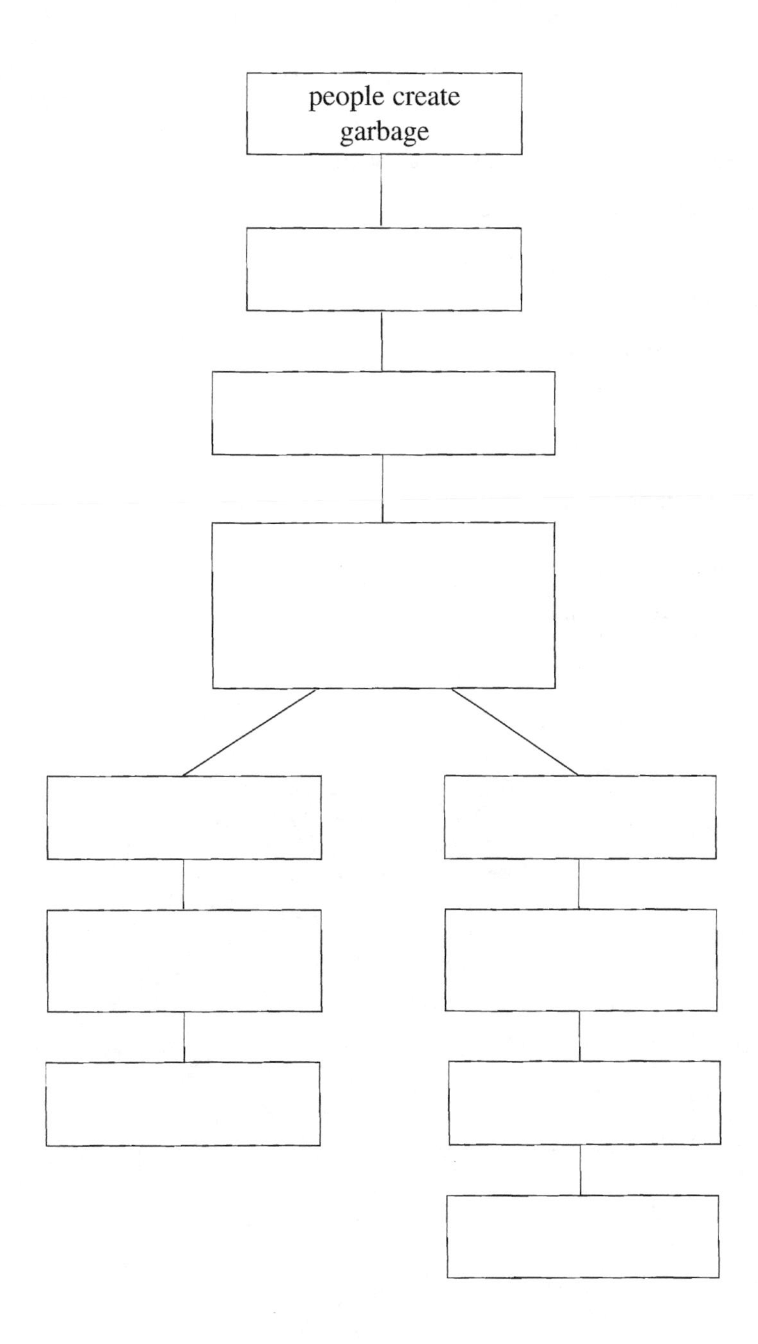

B. *Circle the correct answer.*

1. The Craft Campus is

a. a new high school in Northern California.

b. an art building in the mountains.

c. a place where engineers go to school.

2. The Craft Campus is unusual because

a. it has huge furnaces and ovens.

b. the art studios are large.

c. electricity in the building comes from gas at a garbage dump.

3. A landfill is

a. a place where homes are built.

b. a place where garbage is dumped.

c. a large hole filled with dirt.

4. The partnership between Buncombe County and the university is important because it

a. shows how people in business and education work together.

b. will help to reduce global warming.

c. accelerates global warming.

5. Which is not a ramification of the project?

a. It will help the economy.

b. It will allow more students to study art.

c. It will provide more jobs in furniture manufacturing.

Part 2 *(10 points)*

A. *For each pair of words, circle* **S** *if they are synonyms or* **A** *if they are antonyms.*

1. convinced	unsure	S	A
2. countless	numerous	S	A
3. sacred	cursed	S	A
4. horrify	shock	S	A
5. ramifications	consequences	S	A

B. ***Choose the correct definition or synonym for each underlined word or phrase.***

1. Methane can be a grave danger.

a. dead

b. serious

c. heavy

2. It contributes to accelerating global warming.

a. speeding up

b. slowing down

c. maintaining

3. Conservation groups are convinced that the partnership is vital.

a. observation

b. conservative

c. preservation

4. The trees will prevent the heat from intensifying.

a. decreasing

b. increasing

c. weakening

5. Conservation groups are convinced that the partnership is vital.

a. important

b. insignificant

c. fancy

NAME

Read the article.

Gone but Not Forgotten

Jeanne Louise Calment, born February 21, 1875, had the longest confirmed lifespan in history when she died on August 4, 1997, at 122 years and 164 days. Her lifespan has been documented by scientific study; more records have been produced to verify her age than for any other person. She came from a family who lived long lives: her father died at 93, her mother at 86, and her brother at 97.

Jeanne was born in Arles, a city in the south of France. She reported attending the funeral of French novelist Victor Hugo when she was ten years old. The famous Eiffel Tower was completed in 1889, when Jeanne was just fourteen years old. That same year she met artist Vincent van Gogh. At the age of twenty-one, Jeanne married Fernand Calment. He died in 1942, just four years before their fiftieth wedding anniversary. She lived longer than her daughter and her grandson.

At age ninety she had no living heirs, so she signed an agreement, common in France, to sell her apartment to lawyer François Raffray. Raffray, who was forty-seven at the time, agreed to pay Jeanne a monthly sum until she died. Common sense indicated that Raffray made a good deal because the value of the apartment was equal to ten years of payments. Unfortunately for Raffray, Jeanne lived more than thirty years, and Raffray died first. His widow had to continue the payments.

Jeanne had an extraordinarily active life. When she was 85, she decided to learn fencing, a sport that requires good balance and ease of movement. She was still riding a bicycle with confidence when she was 100 years old. Jeanne lived alone until shortly before her 110th birthday, when she caused an accidental fire in her apartment while cooking. She had to give up living alone, so she moved to a nursing home. She was still in good shape and able to walk until she fell just before her 115th birthday. Jeanne had a hip operation in 1990 and was limited to a wheelchair afterward. Jeanne was a smoker and quit when she was 117 years old, only because she was nearly blind and was embarrassed to ask for a light. When asked on her 120th birthday what kind of future she expected to have, she came up with the perfect answer: "A short one," she said. Regardless of her age, she received frequent visitors until her 122nd birthday, when it was finally decided that her health status had declined and she needed privacy. She died five months later.

Interest in Jeanne and her life peaked in 1988 when the 100-year anniversary of Van Gogh's visit to Arles provided her with an opportunity to meet reporters. At the age of 114, she appeared briefly in the film *Vincent and Me* as herself, making her the oldest actress ever. A documentary film about her life, entitled *Beyond 120 Years with Jeanne Calment,* was released in 1995.

Part I *(10 points)*

A. ***Circle the correct answer.***

1. Which describes Jeanne Calment's attitude about herself?

a. She thought she needed a lot of help.

b. She wanted to be independent as long as she could.

c. She hated being alone.

2. What was Jeanne like at the age of 85?

a. She was slow moving and rather inactive.

b. She probably had serious medical problems.

c. She had good balance and could move easily.

3. Why did Jeanne move to a nursing home?

a. She fell and broke her hip.

b. She accidentally started a fire in her apartment.

c. She was tired of being alone.

4. What was probably Jeanne's attitude about life?

a. Live and play hard and enjoy life to the fullest.

b. Buy and sell as much real estate as possible.

c. Live carefully and don't take too many chances.

5. What did other people most likely think about Jeanne?

a. They really didn't know anything about her.

b. They admired her and thought her life was interesting.

c. They thought she needed a lot of protection.

B. ***Check the statements that are inferences you can make based on the information in the article.***

_____ **1.** Jeanne's decision to sell her apartment benefited her.

_____ **2.** François Raffray's widow was happy about the purchase of the apartment after he died.

_____ **3.** Jeanne Calment was an independent woman.

_____ **4.** Jeanne didn't care what people thought about her.

_____ **5.** Jeanne had a long career as an actress.

Part 2 *(15 points)*

A. ***Circle the letter of the correct answer.***

1. Which person would listen to Jeanne's heart?

a. a climatologist   b. a cardiologist

2. Which person would examine Jeanne's skin?

a. a dermatologist   b. an anthropologist

3. Which person would talk to Jeanne about pain in her legs?

a. a geologist b. a neurologist

4. Which person would be interested in Jeanne's life?

a. a gerontologist b. a geologist

5. Which person would test Jeanne's hearing?

a. an anthropologist b. an audiologist

B. ***Place the letter of the correct answer on the line next to each word.***

1. _____	rich	a. one of the first to do something
2. _____	foremost	b. a rule or idea that has you behave a certain way
3. _____	pioneer	c. belief in your own or someone else's ability
4. _____	principle	d. full
5. _____	confidence	e. most important

C. ***Circle the word or phrase that is closest in meaning to the underlined word or phrase in each sentence.***

1. Jeanne had an <u>extraordinarily</u> active life.

a. extremely

b. understandably

c. minimally

2. Jeanne Calment probably <u>hung out with</u> very active people.

a. worked for

b. looked for

c. spent time with

3. Jeanne's life takes the idea that elderly people are weak and fragile and <u>turns it on its head</u>.

a. looks away

b. makes it the opposite of what it was

c. makes it seem the same

4. At 85 years of age, Jeanne had the <u>endurance</u> to learn fencing.

a. ability to remain strong

b. ability to behave sensibly

c. opportunity

5. At 100 years of age, Jeanne was quite <u>competent</u>.

a. tired

b. skilled

c. confused

UNIT TESTS ANSWER KEY

UNIT 1 TEST

Part 1 A
1. b
2. a
3. c
4. b

Part 1 B
1. T
2. T
3. F
4. F
5. T
6. T

Part 2 A

inconsiderate
illogical
imperfect
impolite
irresponsible

1. imperfect
2. impolite or inconsiderate
3. irresponsible
4. illogical
5. impolite or inconsiderate

Part 2 B

realization
generation
situation
disconnection
consideration

1. generation
2. consideration
3. disconnection
4. situation
5. realization

UNIT 2 TEST

Part 1 A
1. F
2. F
3. F
4. T
5. F
6. F

Part 1 B
1. d
2. f
3. a
4. b
5. c
6. e

Part 2 A
1. c
2. e
3. a
4. f
5. d
6. b

Part 2 B
1. g
2. e
3. f
4. a
5. c
6. d
7. b

UNIT 3 TEST

Part 1 A
1. T
2. F
3. F
4. F
5. T

Part 1 B
1. O
2. O
3. F
4. O
5. F

Part 1 C
1. b
2. a
3. c
4. b

Part 2 A
1. b
2. a
3. b
4. a
5. a

Part 2 B
1. slow
2. extra
3. irritating
4. dull
5. criticize
6. unknown

UNIT 4 TEST

Part 1 A
1. F
2. F
3. O
4. F
5. O
6. O

Part 1 B
1. a. I
   b. M
   c. I
2. a. I
   b. I
   c. M
3 a. M
   b. I
   c. I

Part 2 A
1. b
2. a
3. b
4. a
5. a

Part 2 B
1. Yes
2. Yes
3. No
4. Yes
5. No

UNIT 5 TEST

Part 1 A
1. b
2. c
3. a
4. b
5. c

Part 1 B
1. d
2. a
3. b
4. c
5. e

Part 2
1. carried
2. animals
3. answer
4. insane
5. cooperated

UNIT 6 TEST

Part 1 A
1. ✓
2. ✓
3.
4.
5. ✓

Part 1 B
1. F
2. O
3. F
4. O
5. F

Part 1 C
1. 7
2. $100,000
3. 86
4. 1920
5. 84

Part 2 A
1. facts
2. disinterested
3. banned
4. weird
5. lose

Part 2 B
Answers will vary. Possibilities are:
1. bad luck
2. scam
3. ideas
4. fantasy
5. persist

UNIT 7 TEST

Part 1 A

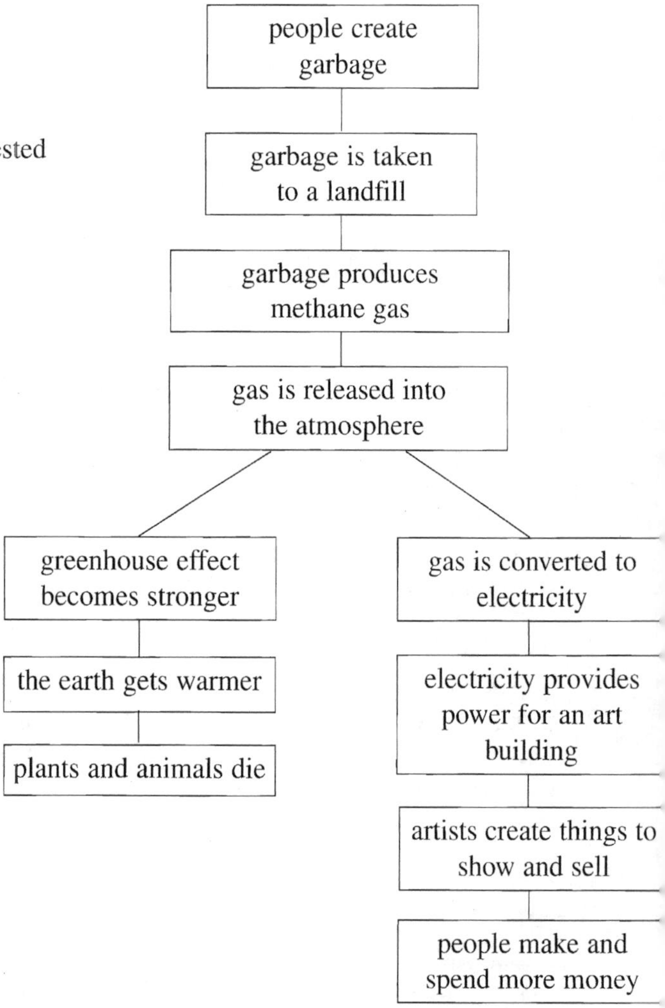

people create garbage
garbage is taken to a landfill
garbage produces methane gas
gas is released into the atmosphere
greenhouse effect becomes stronger
the earth gets warmer
plants and animals die
gas is converted to electricity
electricity provides power for an art building
artists create things to show and sell
people make and spend more money

Part 1 B
1. b
2. c
3. b
4. b
5. c

Part 2 A
1. A
2. S
3. A
4. S
5. S

Part 2 B
1. b
2. a
3. c
4. b
5. a

Part 1 B
1. ✓
2.
3. ✓
4.
5.

Part 2 A
1. b
2. a
3. b
4. a
5. b.

Part 2 B
1. d
2. e
3. a
4. b
5. c

Part 2 C
1. a
2. c
3. b
4. a
5. b

UNIT 8 TEST

Part 1 A
1. b
2. c
3. b
4. a
5. b

STUDENT BOOK ANSWER KEY

UNIT 1

CHAPTER 1

Comprehension Check

A (page 4)

2. T
3. T
4. T
5. F
6. T

B (page 5)

2. c
3. a
4. b

Vocabulary Practice

A (page 6)

2. e
3. g
4. b
5. d
6. a
7. f

B (page 6)

2. documents
3. instead of
4. deal
5. vary
6. associated with
7. represent

C. (page 7)

2. fight
3. discover
4. humans
5. for instance
6. stranger
7. make up

CHAPTER 2

Comprehension Check

A (page 11)

1. T
2. T
3. T
4. F
5. T
6. F

B (page 11)

2. ear grasp
3. fingertips kiss
4. head circle
5. the *wai*

C (page 11)

1. Direct eye contact is considered intimidating.
2. Nodding means "no" in Bulgaria.
3. Thumbs up is a rude gesture in Australia.

Vocabulary Practice

A (page 12)

1. g
2. d
3. f
4. b
5. a
6. h
7. c
8. e

B (page 12)

2. Yes
3. Yes
4. No
5. No
6. Yes
7. No

C (page 13)

-in: inappropriate, inconvenient;
-il: illegal, illiterate;
-im: impolite, impossible;
-ir: irregular, irresponsible

D (page 13)

1. illegal
2. inappropriate
3. illiterate
4. impossible
5. inconvenient
6. irresponsible
7. impolite
8. irregular

CHAPTER 3

Comprehension Check

A (page 17)

1. T
2. T
3. F
4. T
5. F
6. F
7. T

B (page 17)

Hungary: onions, fat, paprika;
Japan: soy sauce, rice wine, sesame, ginger;
Korea: soy sauce, sesame, chili;
Indonesia: soy sauce, peanuts, sugar

Vocabulary Practice

A (page 18)

1. ethnic
2. flavorings
3. complicated
4. cuisine
5. passed down, generation
6. system

C (page 18)

1. a. creation b. create
2. a. realize b. realization
3. a. description b. describe
4. a. combine b. combination
5. a. complicate b. complication

Talk It Over (page 19)

This is a typical day of a relatively typical soul in today's diversified world. I wake up to the sound of my Japanese clock radio, put on a T-shirt sent to me by an uncle in Nigeria, and walk out into the street, past German cars, to my office. Around me are English-language students from Korea, Switzerland, and Argentina—all on this Spanish-named road in this Mediterranean-style town. On TV, I find the news is in Mandarin; today's baseball game is being broadcast in Korean. For lunch, I can walk to a sushi-bar, a tandoori palace, a Thai café, or the latest burrito joint (run by an old Japanese lady). Who am I, I sometimes wonder—the son of Indian parents and a British citizen who spends much of his time in Japan (and is therefore—what else?—an American permanent resident)? And where am I?

I am, as it happens, in Southern California, in a quiet, relatively uninternational town, but I could easily be in Vancouver or Sydney or London or Hong Kong. All the world's a rainbow coalition, more and more; the whole world, you might say, is going global.

Tie It All Together

Just for Fun (page 21)

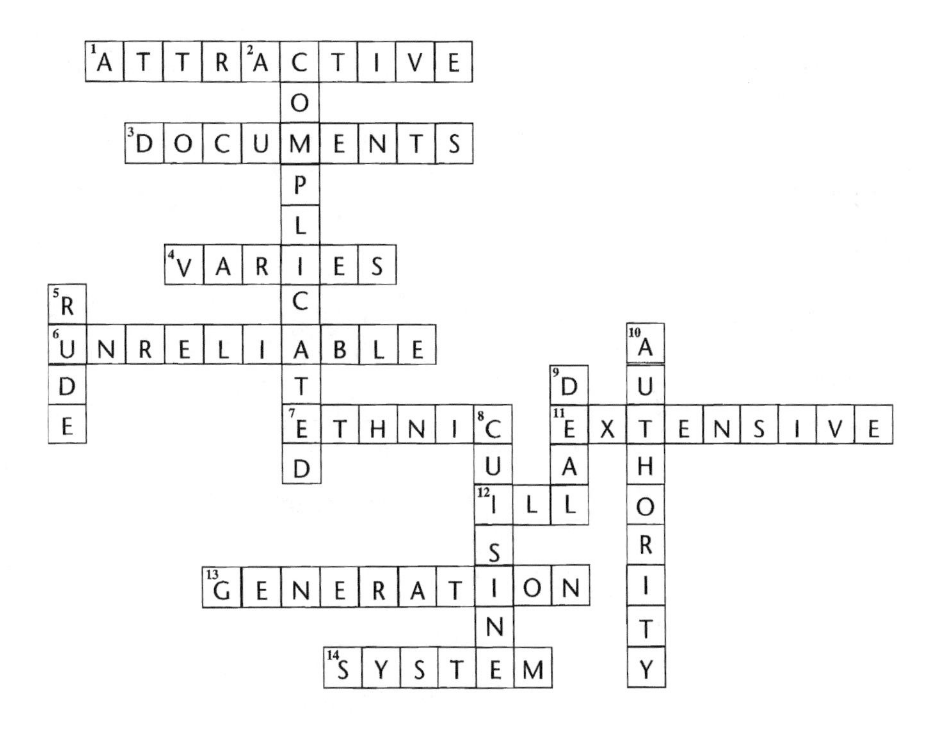

ABC News Video Activity

B (page 22)

1. b
2. c
3. a
4. a
5. c

Vocabulary Self-Test

A (page 23)

1. associated with
2. attractive
3. ethnic
4. signify
5. made up
6. system
7. complicated

B (page 23)

1. cuisine
2. generations
3. vary
4. ill
5. deal
6. documents
7. unreliable

C (page 24)

1. instead of
2. authority
3. rude
4. flavorings
5. pass down
6. appreciation
7. extensive
8. represent

UNIT 2

Chapter 1

Before You Read

B (page 26)

1, 2, 5, 6, 7

Comprehension Check

A (page 29)

1. F
2. T
3. F
4. T
5. F
6. F
7. T

B (page 29)

2. 8
3. 1
4. 4
5. 8
6. 3

C (page 30)

1, 2, 3, 5, 7, 10

Vocabulary Practice

A (page 30)

2. c
3. c
4. b
5. b
6. c
7. a
8. b
9. b
10. b

B (page 32)

2. huge
3. noisy
4. success
5. simple
6. ignore
7. predict
8. confuse
9. archaeologist

C (page 32)

1. d
2. a
3. b
4. e
5. c

D (page 33)

1. coexist
2. cosign
3. coworker
4. coeducational
5. coauthor

Chapter 2

Before You Read

B (page 35)

2

Comprehension Check

A (page 36)

1. c
2. d
3. b
4. a
5. d

B (page 37)

1, 3, 4, 6

C (page 38)

2. in the 1920s
3. 1946
4. 12,000 years
5. 9 miles (15 km)

Vocabulary Practice

A (page 38)

1. d
2. g
3. a
4. b
5. f
6. e
7. c

B (page 38)

1. fact
2. saddened
3. style
4. modern
5. calendar
6. know
7. bore
8. stop

C (page 39)

2. near
3. enormous, giant
4. controversy
5. removed
6. busy
7. approximately

Chapter 3

Comprehension Check

A (page 44)

1. a
2. b
3. c
4. b
5. b

B (page 44)

2, 5, 7, 13

Vocabulary Practice

A (page 45)

1. c
2. e
3. b
4. f
5. a
6. g
7. d

B (page 45)

2. a
3. b
4. b
5. a
6. b
7. a

C (page 46)

1. a
2. b
3. b
4. a
5. a

D (page 47)

2. economist
3. librarian
4. violinist
5. musician
6. magician
7. artist

E (page 48)

1. librarian
2. magician
3. musician
4. economist
5. comedian
6. violinist
7. artist

Tie It All Together

Just for Fun (page 49)

2. Thor
3. pilots
4. mayor
5. mummy
6. theories
7. tattoos
8. silent
9. invention
10. mysteries

ABC News Video Activity

B (page 50)

1. T
2. F
3. T
4. T
5. F
6. T

Vocabulary Self-Test

A (page 51)

1. intrigued
2. speculate
3. estimated
4. biologist
5. sensation

B (page 51)

1. figure out
2. Agriculture
3. weapon
4. on purpose
5. silent
6. fascinate

C (page 52)

1. carve
2. theory
3. belongings
4. disaster
5. tiny
6. shocked

D (page 52)

1. cooperated
2. evidence
3. sparked
4. descendant
5. magnificent
6. baffled

UNIT 3

Chapter 1

Comprehension Check
(page 57)

	Birthplace	Band	Causes/Foundations
Bono	Ireland	U2	AIDS and poverty in Africa; Victims of tsunami in Thailand and of Hurricane Katrina in New Orleans
Ricky Martin	Puerto Rico	Menudo	The Ricky Martin Foundation to help children
Sting	England	The Police	Amnestly International; The Rainforest Foundation

Vocabulary Practice

A (page 57)

1. c
2. g
3. a
4. e
5. f
6. b
7. d
8. i
9. h

B (page 57)

1. charity
2. solo
3. committed
4. cause
5. humanitarian
6. victims
7. accomplished
8. overcome
9. celebrity

C (page 58)

1. a. making money
   b. make ends meet
   c. make an exception
2. a. make a good impression
   b. make up your mind
3. a. make excuses
   b. make a difference
   c. make time

Chapter 2

Before You Read

B (Page 60)

2

Comprehension Check

A (page 62)

1.	F	4.	T
2.	T	5.	F
3.	F	6.	T

B (page 63)

1.	Opinion	6.	Opinion
2.	Fact	7.	Fact
3.	Opinion	8.	Fact
4.	Opinion		
5.	Fact		

Vocabulary Practice

A (page 63)

1.	d	5.	g
2.	e	6.	b
3.	f	7.	a
4.	c		

B (page 64)

1. kick off
2. composer, masterpieces
3. renovated
4. genius
5. delighted
6. praises

C (page 64)

1. homesick
2. workplace
3. keyhole
4. skateboard
5. mastermind
6. nationwide
7. blackboard
8. homework
9. birthrate
10. citywide

Chapter 3

Before You Read

B (page 66)

1, 2, 3, 5

Comprehension Check

A (page 69)

1.	a	5.	c
2.	c	6.	c
3.	c	7.	a
4.	b	8.	c

B (page 70)

Answers may vary.
Facts:
Every day over 100 million people hear the sound of background music.
Background music can affect the sales of a business.
Ronald Milliman is a marketing professor.
Opinions:
Nothing creates experience more powerfully than music.
Muzak is annoying and boring.
Muzak is enjoyable and has a calming effect.

C (page 70)

1.	b	4.	b
2.	c	5.	b
3.	a		

Vocabulary Practice

A (page 71)

1.	a	5.	a
2.	a	6.	b
3.	a	7.	a
4.	b		

B (page 71)

1. slow
2. extra
3. seller
4. patient
5. pleasing
6. annoying
7. boring

C (page 71)

1. requested
2. nearly
3. finish
4. tunes
5. lively
6. claimed
7. relaxing
8. previous

Tie It All Together

Just for Fun (page 73)

1. Steve and Mary
2. Steve: tuba and drums; Mary: saxophone and guitar.
3. John, Carol, Tom, and David
4. John: saxophone; Carol: guitar; Tom: drums; David: tuba

ABC News Video Activity

B (page 74)

1, 3, 5, 4, 2

Vocabulary Self-Test

A (page 75)

1. lively
2. client
3. inspirational
4. solo
5. kick off
6. renovate
7. accomplished
8. celebrity

B (page 75)

1. patient
2. composers
3. praised
4. charities
5. genius
6. essential
7. overcome

C (page 76)

1. cause
2. victims

3. annoying
4. humanitarian
5. delighted
6. masterpiece
7. calming
8. committed

UNIT 4

Chapter 1

Comprehension Check

A (page 81)

1. b
2. b
3. c
4. b

B (page 81)

1. T
2. T
3. F
4. T
5. F
6. F

C (Page 82)

Fad	Creator	Date	Description
the Hula Hoop	Arthur Melin and Richard Knerr	1958	a big hoop of colorful plastic
Beanie Babies	Ty Warner	1993	soft, small, stuffed animals
Silly Putty	scientists at GE; Peter Hodgson	1944 1949	a rubberlike material that can bounce and stretch
the Slinky	Richard James	1945	a long piece of flat, coiled wire
the Mood Ring	Joshua Reynolds	1975	rings with stones that can turn blue, green, black, or brown
the Pet Rock	Gary Dahl	1975	a rock with an instruction manual

Vocabulary Practice

A (page 82)

1. d
2. a
3. c
4. b
5. f
6. h
7. e
8. g

B (page 82)

1. sold like hotcakes
2. invested
3. word of mouth
4. practical
5. make a mint
6. tips
7. mood
8. catches on

Chapter 2

Before You Read

B (page 85)

2

Comprehension Check

A (page 87)

1. b
2. a
3. c
4. a
5. c
6. a

B (page 88)

1. Opinion
2. Fact
3. Fact
4. Opinion
5. Opinion
6. Fact

Vocabulary Practice

A (page 89)

1. vehicles
2. stinks
3. fuel
4. alternative
5. flexible
6. run out of
7. convert

B (page 89)

1. Yes
2. Yes
3. No
4. Yes
5. Yes
6. Yes
7. Yes

C (page 90)

1. profitable
2. usable
3. solvable
4. convertible
5. renewable
6. predictable
7. exhaustible

D (page 90)

1. exhaustible
2. renewable
3. predictable
4. solvable
5. usable
6. convertible
7. profitable

CHAPTER 3

Comprehension Check

A (page 94)

1.	T	5.	F
2.	T	6.	T
3.	T	7.	F
4.	F	8.	T

B (page 95)

2. M, S, S
3. S, M, S
4. S, M, S
5. S, M, S
6. M, S, S
7. S, M, S

Vocabulary Practice

A (page 97)

1.	e	5.	f
2.	a	6.	d
3.	g	7.	b
4.	c		

B (page 97)

1.	a	5.	b
2.	b	6.	a
3.	a	7.	b
4.	a		

C (page 97)

1. real
2. confusion
3. sound
4. easy
5. lead by the nose

D (page 98)

1.	b	4.	c
2.	c	5.	b
3.	a	6.	a

E (page 99)

1. smells fishy
2. smell a rat
3. wake up and smell the coffee
4. pass the smell test
5. came out smelling like a rose

TIE IT ALL TOGETHER

Just for Fun (page 101)

Answers will vary.

1.	car	7.	crave
2.	star	8.	roar
3.	rat	9.	rare
4.	rail	10.	late
5.	art	11.	vane
6.	train	12.	soar

ABC News Video Activity

B (page 102)

Wording of answers may vary.

1. A style becomes a trend very quickly. If a famous person (such as an actor or singer) wears something new, other people will immediately start wearing it to emulate that person and appear fashionable and trendy.
2. Malcolm Gladwell is a best-selling author who studies trends among teens. By saying that "trends are a virus" he means that a trend starts with one person who can influence others to copy it. Then it spreads fast from that one person to other people.
3. A trend that relates to speech is called "valley-speak." It started among Australian surfers in the 1960s and was picked up by teenagers who wanted to emulate them.
4. An "it girl" is a girl who is popular among friends and starts new trends. The fashion industry relies on "it girls" because they can easily influence other teenagers to popularize a new trend.

Vocabulary Self-Test

A (page 103)

1. tricky
2. vehicle
3. invested, make a mint
4. fragrance
5. mood
6. fuel

B (page 103)

1. run out of
2. enticed
3. alternative
4. Word of mouth
5. practical
6. tips
7. volunteer
8. selling like hot cakes

C (page 104)

1. proof
2. fake
3. catching on
4. convert
5. stinks
6. led by the nose
7. flexible

UNIT 5

CHAPTER 1

Before You Read

B (page 106)

3

Comprehension Check

A (page 108)

1. c
2. b
3. c
4. a
5. a

B (page 109)

1. nineteenth century
2. 1928
3. 1930s

4. 1939
5. 170,000
6. 2.5 million
7. 10 million
8. 1953
9. 1996

Vocabulary Practice

A (page 110)

1. b
2. a
3. c
4. b
5. a
6. c

B (page 110)

1. trial
2. separates
3. grow
4. failure
5. hold
6. failure

C (page 111)

1. b. something that is related to something else; noun
2. a. to make a change to a musical instrument so it plays correctly; verb
   b. song; noun
3. a. a machine for watching TV; noun
   b. to make something ready; verb
4. a. the flat glass part of a TV or computer; noun
   b. to find out who is calling so you don't have to speak to someone you don't want to talk to; verb
5. a. to store something on video so you can look at it later; verb
   b. information that is written down or stored in a computer so you can look at it later; noun
6. a. to send out a radio or TV show; verb
   b. the mixture of gases that we breathe; noun
7. a. a small clock that you wear on your wrist; noun
   b. look at; verb

Debate the Issue
(page 113)

Answers may vary.

The Television Debate		
	Praise for Television	**Criticism of Television**
1.	great teacher	blamed for poor reading and writing skills of the population
2.	helps understand people around the world	destroys family life
3.	gives information about political issues	we only know short news briefs

CHAPTER 2

Comprehension Check

A (page 118)

1. b
2. a
3. c
4. a
5. a
6. b
7. c

Vocabulary Practice

A (page 119)

1. prime time
2. animated
3. characters
4. heroine
5. theme
6. spin-off
7. episode
8. pilot
9. diversity

B (page 120)

1. f
2. g
3. d
4. a
5. c
6. b
7. e
8. h
9. i

C (page 120)

1. bicycle
2. multimillionaire
3. multicolored
4. bilateral
5. multimedia
6. bifocals
7. multilateral
8. bipeds
9. multifaceted

CHAPTER 3

Comprehension Check

A (page 124)

1. T
2. F
3. F
4. F
5. F
6. T
7. F
8. T

B (page 125)

Type	Definition/ Explanation	Examples
1. contest-based	real people compete for a prize based on certain skills	a. *Survivor* b. *American Idol* c. *The Bachelor*
2. self-improvement	real people attempt to improve a specific area of their lives	a. *Extreme Makeover* b. *The Biggest Loser*
3. documentary-style	camera follows regular people going about their daily lives in an artificially created situation	a. *The Real World* b. *Big Brother* c. *Wife Swap*

Vocabulary Practice

A (page 125)

1. c
2. b
3. a
4. c
5. a
6. b
7. c

B (page 126)

1. producer
2. return
3. create
4. size
5. attach
6. discuss

C (page 126)

2. tiredness
3. illness
4. kindness
5. laziness
6. leadership
7. membership
8. partnership
9. selfishness
10. sportsmanship

D (page 127)

1. illness
2. leadership
3. selfishness
4. sportsmanship
5. partnership
6. membership
7. laziness
8. kindness
9. companionship
10. tiredness

Tie It All Together

Just for Fun (page 128)

S	Y	Y	O	A	C	T	S	A	T	Y	S	C	T	H
C	L	R	M	V	S	R	E	X	T	E	T	A	C	L
S	J	A	L	L	N	Z	T	Z	I	U	R	R	B	P
R	R	T	I	K	J	P	N	R	F	J	O	T	C	R
D	O	N	Z	C	P	V	E	O	O	X	P	O	Z	O
B	O	E	W	O	R	T	I	D	I	C	S	O	F	A
O	V	M	I	B	S	E	O	D	O	T	C	N	B	Y
N	E	U	C	Y	G	O	M	J	E	V	C	S	J	C
O	H	C	M	M	I	F	F	M	J	O	C	A	O	Y
E	G	O	D	B	O	I	R	H	O	K	T	M	F	R
L	R	D	N	E	W	S	J	R	K	C	E	A	D	N
S	A	T	E	L	L	I	T	E	F	D	F	T	P	Q
E	S	N	Y	R	B	D	H	B	I	U	J	Q	E	E
A	E	W	V	O	N	Q	B	E	K	P	W	F	O	S
A	P	S	N	R	E	T	S	E	W	H	D	A	W	X

ABC News Video Activity

B (page 129)

Wording of answers may vary.

2. The American Academy of Pediatrics recommends no TV for children under two because it is not known how TV can affect young children.
3. The recommendation is not based on experiments with children because there isn't enough research on how TV affects very young children.
4. Most parents don't know how to interact with their kids when they watch TV. The new DVD shows parents how to interact with their kids while watching the program.

5. The best way for children to learn is not by watching TV. The best way for them to learn is through interactive play.

Vocabulary Self-Test

A (page 131)

1. Animated
2. brought a halt to
3. character
4. linked
5. big hit
6. remodel
7. contestant

B (page 131)

1. heroine
2. transmitted
3. pilot, theme
4. craze
5. swap
6. categories
7. documentary

C (page 132)

1. spin-off
2. Prime-time
3. episode
4. trial and error
5. eliminated
6. critique
7. interfere
8. diversity

UNIT 6

CHAPTER 1

Comprehension Check

A (page 136)

1. 7
2. 4
3. 3
4. 2
5. 5

B (page 137)

1, 3, 5, 6

C (page 137)

1. fear of the number 13
2. many Asian countries
3. *I lived* (or *I'm dead*)
4. the word for *to acquire wealth*
5. 8 P.M. on August 8

Vocabulary Practice

A (page 137)

1. rearrange, skip
2. banned, security
3. acquired
4. feast
5. notion

B (page 138)

1. b
2. b
3. b
4. b
5. a
6. b
7. a

C (page 138)

1. fact
2. add
3. allow
4. exercise
5. concern
6. lose

D (page 139)

1. a. a line of things or people next to each other; noun
   b. make a boat move; verb
2. a. not to do something even though it is the next logical thing; verb
   b. move forward with quick jumps from one foot to another; verb
3. a. a small round object on a machine that you push to make it work; noun
   b. to fasten; verb
4. a. to hit something with your foot so that you fall or almost fall; verb
   b. an occasion when you go from one place to another; a journey; noun
5. a. a piece of paper, metal, etc., in a public place that gives information such as directions or prices; noun
   b. to write your name; verb

Reading Further
(page 140)

Food	Superstition	Place of Origin	Effect
2. rice	throw rice at weddings	Europe	calm evil spirits
3. salt	throw salt on door of new house	Hungary	protect from evil spirits
4. mustard seed	put mustard seed on roof	Europe	keep vampires away
5. beans	put beans in dark corners and entrances of house	Japan	drive out evil spirits
6. garlic	put garlic around the neck or over doors	Europe	charm against evil spirits

Chapter 2

Before You Read

B (page 141)

1

Comprehension Check

A (page 143)

1. to help them guarantee a victory or make sure they won't get hurt
2. to provide the illusion of control
3. uniforms, food, numbers

B (page 144)

Athlete	Sport	Superstition
1. Tiger Woods	golf	wears red on the last day of a tournament
2. Michael Jordan	basketball	always wore his blue North Carolina shorts under his Chicago Bulls uniform
3. Mario Andretti	racing	wouldn't enter a car from the right side
4. Wayne Gretzsky	hockey	won't get his hair cut when his team plays away games
5. Ronnie Lott	football	wears lucky shorts under his uniform; always eats a hamburger the night before a game
6. Joe Louis	boxing	had to put his left boxing glove on first
7. Turk Wendell	baseball	brushed his teeth and ate licorice between every inning
8. Nomar Garciapara	baseball	gets dressed the same way; steps on each step of the dugout with both feet, and taps his toes when its his turn to bat
9. Wade Boggs	baseball	ate chicken before every game; ran in outfield at 7:17 every day
10. Jose Mercedes	baseball	wouldn't pitch in the third game of a season
11. Tony La Russa	baseball	prints the names of the players' batting order every game until they lose; then, switches to cursive writing; when St. Louis loses again, goes back to printing
12. Mark von Eeghen	football	to protect himself from injury, would climb atop the television in his hotel room and jump to the bed

C (page 145)

1. Fact
2. Opinion
3. Fact
4. Opinion
5. Fact
6. Opinion
7. Fact
8. Opinion

Vocabulary Practice

A (page 145)

1. g
2. c
3. f
4. b
5. d
6. e
7. a

B (page 146)

1. illusion
2. quirk
3. pass up
4. weird
5. hung up on
6. ritual
7. stick to

C (page 146)

1. S
2. A
3. A
4. S
5. S
6. A
7. S

Chapter 3

Comprehension Check

A (page 150)

1. F
2. T
3. T
4. T
5. F
6. T
7. F
8. T

B (page 151)

Answers may vary.

1. objects
2. places
3. bad luck
4. the Hope Diamond
5. legend
6. it would be cursed with bad luck and death
7. King Tutankhamen's tomb
8. enter the tomb will die

Vocabulary Practice

A (page 151)

1. a
2. b
3. a
4. a
5. a
6. b
7. b

B (page 152)

1. something that brings bad luck
2. going to a place in large numbers
3. a piece of writing set on a stone
4. an action of deceiving someone
5. people who ruled in Egypt
6. a surprising situation when two things happen at the same time by chance

C (page 153)

1. S
2. S
3. A
4. S
5. A
6. S

Tie It All Together

Just for Fun (page 154)

3. Raiders
4. seven
5. normal
6. LaRussa
7. Asia
8. a bat
9. tomorrow
10. Washington D.C.

ABC News Video Activity

B (page 155)

1. d
2. e
3. a
4. b
5. c

Vocabulary Self-Test

A (page 156)

1. misfortune
2. stick to
3. security
4. acquired
5. legend
6. hoax
7. hung up on

B (page 156)

1. illusion
2. weird, quirks
3. pass up
4. eager
5. feast
6. rituals

C (page 157)

1. notion, skipping
2. reputation
3. rearranged
4. banned
5. blamed
6. tragedy

UNIT 7

CHAPTER 1

Comprehension Check
(page 163)

1. Yes
2. Yes
3. No
4. Yes
5. No
6. No
7. No
8. Yes
9. Yes

Vocabulary Practice

A (page 164)

1. b
2. c
3. a, a
4. b
5. c
6. b
7. c

B (page 165)

1. a
2. b
3. b
4. a
5. a
6. b
7. a
8. a

C (page 165)

1. a. to put your foot down on something; verb
   b. a flat, narrow surface for climbing up or down; noun
2. a. to show something to someone by holding a finger toward it; verb
   b. the main idea; noun
3. a. the ground; noun
   b. moved down onto the ground; verb
4. a. to force someone to experience something unpleasant; verb
   b. topic; noun
5. a. a period of time when you can relax or sleep; noun
   b. to support an object or put a part of your body on or against something; verb

CHAPTER 2

Comprehension Check

A (page 170)

1. b
2. c
3. a
4. b
5. a
6. b

B (page 171)

1. a. poaching
   b. competition with humans for land
2. a. we lose plants that could feed us
   b. we lose medicinal benefits
3. a. destroying habitats
   b. overhunting
   c. pollution

Vocabulary Practice

A (page 172)

1. d
2. b
3. e
4. f
5. a
6. g
7. c

B (page 172)

1. vanish
2. microscopic
3. accelerate
4. habitat
5. tragic
6. wildlife
7. chain reaction

C (page 173)

1. the scientific study of very small living things
2. small piece of silicon used in computers and other machines
3. an extremely small living creature that cannot be seen without a microscope
4. electrical equipment used for making voices sound louder
5. short electrical wave used for cooking food, sending radio messages, and in radar
6. scientific equipment that makes extremely small things appear larger

D (page 173)

1. microchip
2. microorganism, microscope
3. microphone
4. microbiology
5. microwave

Write a Summary
(page 174)

1. The UN created a plan to help save elephants from becoming extinct.
2. Several African countries want to start selling ivory again.
3. They want to help their countries' economies.

CHAPTER 3

Comprehension Check

A (page 177)

1. a
2. b
3. a
4. a
5. b

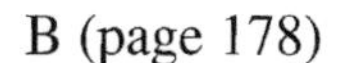
B (page 178)

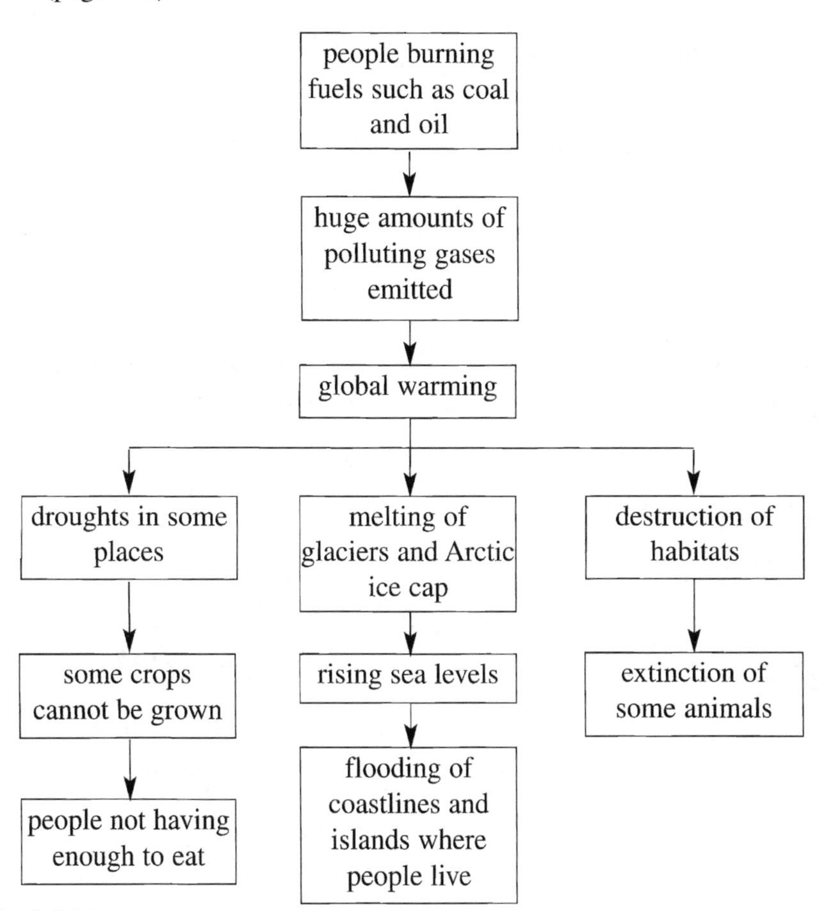

C (page 179)

1. Most scientists who study climate think the Earth is getting warmer.
2. Human behavior is making the trend worse.
3. Rainfall, animal habitats, glaciers, and sea levels are all affected.
4. Reducing the amount of greenhouse gases we put into the atmosphere would slow the effects.

Vocabulary Practice

A (page 179)

1. grave
2. convinced
3. countless
4. treaty
5. vital
6. pledge
7. intensify

B (page 180)

1.	S	5.	S
2.	S	6.	A
3.	A	7.	A
4.	S		

C (page 180)

1.	d	4.	e
2.	a	5.	b
3.	c		

D (page 181)

2. Droughts occur in some places because the Earth's temperature increases.
   OR
   The Earth's temperature increases; therefore, droughts occur in some places.
3. Polluting gases are produced because humans burn fuels.
   OR
   Humans burn fuels; therefore, polluting gases are produced.
4. Birds can't lay healthy eggs because they eat poisoned fish.
   OR
   Birds eat poisoned fish; therefore, they can't lay healthy eggs.
5. Sea levels rise because glaciers melt.
   OR
   Glaciers melt; therefore, sea levels rise.

TIE IT ALL TOGETHER

Just for Fun (page 182)

Answers may vary.

1.	environment	8.	late
2.	man	9.	vent
3.	metal	10.	marine
4.	live	11.	love
5.	tan	12.	trail
6.	role	13.	trial
7.	iron	14.	train

ABC News Video Activity

B (page 183)

1.	a	3.	c
2.	a	4.	c

Vocabulary Self-Test

A (page 184)

1. conquests
2. habitats, species
3. treaty
4. countless
5. tragic
6. convince
7. stick up for

B (page 184)

1. conscious
2. conservation
3. chain reaction

4. grave
5. accelerated
6. fancy
7. vital

C (page 185)

1. pledge
2. sacred
3. horrifying
4. wildlife
5. microscopic
6. vanished
7. ramifications
8. intensify

UNIT 8

Chapter 1

Comprehension Check

A (page 191)

1. T
2. F
3. T
4. T
5. T
6. F
7. T

B

1, 2, 3, 4, 5, 6, 8, 10

Vocabulary Practice

A (page 192)

1. a, c
2. b
3. b
4. a
5. a
6. c
7. c

B (page 193)

2. cardiology, cardiologist
3. dermatology, dermatologist
4. neurology, neurologist
5. geology, geologist
6. climatology, climatologist

Chapter 2

Comprehension Check

A (page 197)

1. a
2. b
3. a
4. b
5. a
6. c

B (page 198)

1. Fact
2. Opinion
3. Opinion
4. Opinion
5. Fact
6. Fact
7. Fact
8. Opinion
9. Fact

Vocabulary Practice

A (page 198)

1. e
2. c
3. a
4. f
5. g
6. d
7. b

B (page 199)

1. b
2. a
3. a
4. b
5. a
6. b
7. a

C (page 199)

1. c
2. d
3. b
4. a
5. f
6. e

D (page 200)

1. learn by heart, keep your chin up, break a leg
2. see eye to eye, have cold feet, keep your lips sealed

Chapter 3

Comprehension Check

A (page 203)

1. T
2. F
3. T
4. F
5. T
6. F
7. T
8. F

B (page 204)

1, 4, 6, 7

Vocabulary Practice

A (page 204)

1. b
2. a
3. c
4. a
5. b

B (page 205)

1. looking forward to
2. coming down with
3. looked up to
4. got around to, put up with
5. look down on

Read a Graph

(page 205)

1. 1900
2. 1950
3. 20
4. 65

Tie It All Together

ABC News Video Activity

B (page 207)

a

Vocabulary Self-Test

A (page 208)

1. fatigue
2. rich
3. toddlers
4. regardless
5. confidence
6. come up with
7. endurance

B (page 208)

1. pioneers
2. quest
3. plain
4. gave up
5. hang out with
6. principle
7. concentrate

C (page 209)

1. feat
3. competent, common sense
3. foremost
4. turned it on its head
5. extraordinarily
6. peak

THE FYI DVD PROGRAM

ABOUT THE FYI DVD PROGRAM

The DVD

The FYI 3 and 4 DVD Program includes 16 video segments featuring topics correlated to the themes in FYI Levels 3 and 4.

Scripts for Level 3

Unit 1	Personal Space
Unit 2	Easter Island
Unit 3	Wynton Marsalis
Unit 4	Teen Trends
Unit 5	Baby TV
Unit 6	The Pharaoh's Curse
Unit 7	The Eagles Return
Unit 8	Longevity Gene?

The DVD Guide

The FYI 3 and 4 DVD Guide contains unit-by-unit video scripts as well as vocabulary for comprehension and a summary statement to enhance the accessibility and enjoyment of the DVD material.

DVD Activities

Video Activities are included at the end of every Student Book unit. The activities are designed for students to use in class after watching the video segment.

Using the FYI DVD Program

Preparation

Before presenting a DVD unit to students:

1. Preview the video.
2. Read the video script, along with the summary statement and Vocabulary for Comprehension sections. You may want to take notes to plan how to prepare students for viewing the video.

Procedure

This three-phase procedure takes about 45 minutes to complete.

Before Viewing **Suggested Time: 10 minutes**

1. Introduce the topic to the students. Share the background information provided in the DVD Guide or in the Student Book activity. Draw attention to how this topic relates to the theme in the FYI Student Book units.
2. Generate interest. Find out what students know about this topic and what they think they may learn.
3. Preview vocabulary. Write the words listed in the Vocabulary for Comprehension section

on the board. Review these words. Provide examples to illustrate the meanings of the remaining words, for example, use pictures, situations, synonyms, or antonyms.

Variation

You may choose to go over the meanings of the words after students have viewed the video segment the first time and have heard the words in context.

While Viewing **Suggested Time: 20 minutes**

1. Have students predict. Show a short portion of the video. Use the pause control to stop the DVD. Ask students what they think the rest of the segment will be about. You may write the ideas on the board.

   Variations

   - Use the pause control to stop after a particular line of dialogue and have students predict the next line.
   - With audio off: Have students predict the content based on viewing a short segment without the sound.
   - With picture off: Have students predict what they will see by listening to the sound without watching the picture.

2. Check comprehension. Show the complete video segment. Have students answer comprehension questions you devise. Encourage students to take notes. Have students compare their answers in pairs and then share them as a class. If students demonstrate a desire to view the video in order to clarify a question, show that particular portion of the video.

   Variations

   - Freeze-frame the entire video segment frame-by-frame by using the pause button and check students' understanding.
   - For detailed listening comprehension practice, copy and distribute a portion of the video script, blanking out selected words. Have students fill in the missing words.

After Viewing **Suggested Time: 15 minutes**

1. Share reactions and opinions on the topic. Go back to the ideas students generated before viewing the video. Were their predictions accurate?
2. Consider some of the suggested activities below.

   Speaking Activities

   - Oral summary: Have students work in pairs to summarize the content of the video. Have pairs present their summaries to the class.
   - Role play: Give students various roles of people portrayed in the video. Have students improvise conversations, interviews, or panel discussions based on what they saw in the video.
   - Debate: Have students examine both sides of an issue raised in the video. Divide the class into two groups, pro and con, and have the groups present contrasting viewpoints.
   - Critical review: Have students review the video segment as critics. Have them describe what they liked or didn't like, and what they would change and why.
   - Oral research report: Have students search in the library or on the Internet for more information on the person, place, or issue covered in the video and present an oral report to the class.
   - Survey: Have each student create an opinion or personal experience question related to the topic in the video. Have students circulate and ask each other their questions. Report results to the whole class.

Writing Activities

- Note taking: Have students practice note taking skills as they watch the video segment.
- Paraphrasing: Have students paraphrase selected portions of the video script.
- Summarizing: Have students write a short summary of the video segment. Encourage students to use terms from the Vocabulary for Comprehension section.
- Expository writing: Have students write about an aspect of the video topic that interests them or that they agree or disagree with.
- Critical review: Have students write a review of the video segment. Have them describe what they liked or disliked, and what they would change and why.
- Letter: Have students write a letter to one of the "experts" or people portrayed in the video segment.
- Research report: Have students search in the library or on the Internet for more information on the person, place, or issue covered in the video segment. Have students write outlines and then complete written reports.

FYI 3 VIDEO SCRIPTS

UNIT 1: CROSS-CULTURAL CONNECTIONS

Personal Space
2:51 minutes

Lara Spencer: Personal space, everybody has their own boundaries. But we wondered if there would be a different limit in different parts of the country. I visited malls in New York, Georgia, and Arizona to test, how close is too close? First experiment, the food court.

There are plenty of tables to choose from. So, what happens when a total stranger, me, sits right next to you?

So, you're not leaving because of me, are you?

Woman: No. Oh, no. Not at all.

Lara Spencer: Do you, do you guys mind if I sit here? They're—they're deserting me.

Man: No.

Lara Spencer: Hi. Anybody sitting here?

This New Yorker cannot get away from me fast enough. But in Georgia, it's a different story.

Did I invade your space?

Woman: No. We're pretty friendly.

Lara Spencer: And in Arizona?

Woman: 'Cause I figured the place is full, where are you gonna go? I mean, right. I didn't . . .

Lara Spencer: Even though you saw empty tables there, empty table there?

Woman: Oh, I didn't look, I didn't look over there.

Lara Spencer: Arizona's tally? Seventy-five percent said I did not invade their space. And down South? One hundred percent of the people tested said, y'all come closer, you hear? But in New York, they were not afraid to give their opinion.

Man: And that sit down right in the middle of somebody's conversation, it isn't just an invasion of space, it's a, a lack of consideration and respect.

Lara Spencer: If you're wondering what the tape is for, each of these marks defines what psychologists call the different boundaries of personal space. If I'm standing here and you're over here on the far one, that's five feet. That's public space. If I move here, two feet away from you, now I'm in your personal space. And one step closer, six inches away from you, I'm in your intimate space.

Do you buy into this whole global warming thing? Do you . . .

We told people I was interviewing them on global warming. But as I moved from public to personal to intimate space, we measured the spot where they finally felt it was too hot to handle.

What do you think? Twelve, thirteen inches apart? About thirty and a half? Eighteen inches apart?

Arizona's comfort zone levels were as vast as the Grand Canyon, ranging from ten to thirty-one inches. But the average personal space for Arizonians is twenty inches.

Woman: You know, I have this philosophy. If you—if you grow up in a crowded area, say New York City, space is very important. If you grow up in Georgia, space is not quite as important because it's not invaded as much.

Lara Spencer: So, is she right? The average for Georgia was unanimously a rather close ten inches.

And as for New York?

Am I in your personal space right now?

Man: Yeah. Really, you are.

Lara Spencer: Yeah. I am? What do you think, twenty-seven inches? You got big boundaries.

Those in the Big Apple need big space. The average? Twenty-five point five inches.

Sorry. Am I bothering you?

Woman: You're stepping in my space.

UNIT 2: MYSTERIES FROM THE PAST

Easter Island

2:41 minutes

Darren Abrahamson: Mom, I see it. The whole island is just a big mountain.

Charles Gibson: For 10-year-old Darren and his mom, the 18-hour flight, 18 hours to Easter Island in the South Pacific is just about over.

Darren Abrahamson: Look at this. This is awesome. That's cool.

Charles Gibson: The Chilean island the locals call Rapa Nui is 2,500 miles from the mainland . . .

Darren Abrahamson: Whoa.

Charles Gibson: . . . and is one of the most remote places on earth. Darren was greeted by the locals who adorned him with flowers.

Easter Island Native: Welcome to Rapa Nui.

Charles Gibson: They said they were honored to meet him. Less than 4,000 people live here in the middle of nowhere. Onboard his flight were the Mejias twins. They are two-week-old identical baby boys born on the mainland, because Easter Island has only one incubator. And Darren said he loves babies.

Darren Abrahamson: He's little.

Charles Gibson: His mother says he's fascinated by their faces.

Anna Abrahamson: There's something about babies that really touches Darren's heart.

Darren Abrahamson: Oh, hi. I didn't see you there.

Charles Gibson: After meeting the twins, Darren wanted to see the statues, the majestic Moais, relics from centuries ago made by man long before modern technology.

Darren Abrahamson: Mom, this is so cool. This is awesome.

Charles Gibson: Each statue tells its own story of war, civilization. They represent the history of life on the island.

Darren Abrahamson: So are these carvings of like, people, or . . .?

Anna Abrahamson: Yep.

Darren Abrahamson: So people actually looked like that?

Anna Abrahamson: Mm-hmm.

Darren Abrahamson: Oh, weird.

Charles Gibson: How the statues were moved to the shoreline has fascinated historians and archaeologists. But there's myth that says maybe a higher power lifted them. Darren clambered and climbed and was amazed by each peek at history. He loved seeing everything. Well, almost everything. He, too, was reminded of his illness, his fragile vision, the fact that he's slowly going blind.

Darren Abrahamson: I can't help it, Mom.

Charles Gibson: Looking toward the bright sky was painful. The sunglasses helped. Darren and his mom saw long-sleeping volcanoes, caves, statues and a traffic jam of horses.

Darren Abrahamson: Hey there, horsey.

What's that big stone right over there?

Charles Gibson: He told us that before he totally loses sight that this was what he wanted to see.

Darren Abrahamson: The spiders like it up here, don't they?

Charles Gibson: His mother says she hopes that the magical history might even rub off on Darren's future. The locals say they were touched, moved by Darren's visit, that his presence blessed them.

UNIT 3: MUSIC TO MY EARS

Wynton Marsalis

3:43 minutes

Peter Jennings: This is Wynton Marsalis, one of the most recognizable artists of the late twentieth century, a major life force in American jazz, and on Monday night, jazz in America moved into a new home.

Wynton Marsalis: My goal for this new home and our goal, *Jazz at Lincoln Center's* goal, and the goal of jazz music, is to raise the consciousness of our nation, and ultimately, to bring people together.

Peter Jennings: Wynton Marsalis is the driving force behind *Jazz at Lincoln Center* here in New York City, music capital of the world.

Wynton Marsalis: Welcome to the House of Swing.

Peter Jennings: The House of Swing, and blues and Dixieland and the other forms of jazz, which is, more than any other form, America's contribution to the world of music. It's a $128 million concert theater they have, with three different venues, two music theaters and a nightclub dedicated solely to jazz.

Wynton Marsalis: There have never been halls like the ones we've designed here. These are halls in which the acoustic principles are designed specifically for jazz, to accommodate the high pitch of the, of the cymbal ringing with the bass.

Peter Jennings: It is something of a risk, this new, expensive home. Jazz is struggling in a commercial sense. It is more widely popular in Europe than here, where it was born. Jazz grew out of the black experience in the South, and even as it spread to places like Chicago and Kansas City and New York, it was often played and appreciated in humbler, more intimate settings. The new home for *Jazz at Lincoln Center* is not humble at all, surrounded by a five-star hotel and a midtown shopping mall. Marsalis thinks this may be an advantage.

Wynton Marsalis: We all congregate here because of the energy of the city and the diversity of the people. It's the perfect place for jazz music.

Peter Jennings: Wynton Marsalis is now the biggest star in the world of jazz, sought after by everyone, everywhere. He grew up in New Orleans, where jazz was born.

Wynton Marsalis: The greatest influence on me growing up was my father. He's a jazz musician.

Peter Jennings: Wynton joined the great Art Blakey's band, Jazz Messengers, when he was still a teenager. By 1983, he was the first recording artist ever to win the Grammy for jazz and classical in the same year. In 1997, he won the Pulitzer Prize for music. He and his orchestra, Jazz at Lincoln Center, have played and preached the gospel of this great music all over the world. He is a great and committed educator.

Wynton Marsalis: Jazz, above all else, is a music of communication, of listening and of speaking, because both are required for communication. You have to be a master listener and a master speaker.

Peter Jennings: Marsalis turned 43 on Monday. He lives with his three sons not far from work. He never seems to stop.

Wynton Marsalis: This is a time for us to become a part of the best of what America actually is, and deal with the ascendance of our culture through the spirit of jazz.

UNIT 4: GETTING DOWN TO BUSINESS

Teen Trends
4:06 minutes

Bill Weir: Have you ever wondered why all the kids have to have that particular pair of jeans at this particular point in time? They're trendy, sure. But who decides? Is there an alpha-teen out there somewhere single-handedly determining what is fashionable for the rest of us? Well for this week's *Sensible Shopper,* I went on the hunt for the origins of cool and found an entire industry already on safari.

Pick a trend. Any trend. Low-rise jeans. Black nail polish. Ugg boots. How about the von Dutch trucker's cap? Here's a look that went from truckers to hipsters to Ashton Kutcher to every young head in America to the discount rack. The rise and fall wasn't spontaneous. So someone, somewhere must have been the first to decide it was cool, right?

Malcolm Gladwell: Absolutely.

Bill Weir: Best-selling author Malcolm Gladwell studies this very thing.

Malcolm Gladwell: One of the rare, wonderful cases where we have done this kind of epidemiological work on a trend is "valley-speak." Where they engage in what's called "up-talk." You know how teens talk and they end every sentence like a question even when it's not a question?

Bill Weir: Think the movie *Clueless.*

Actress 1: Hello. There was a stop sign.

Actress 2: I totally paused.

Malcolm Gladwell: It appears to have started among Australian surfers in the '60s. A group of Australian surfers would then come to southern California, and all kinds of little teeny-boppers would cluster around them and try to emulate them.

Bill Weir: "Trends are a virus," Gladwell says. And somewhere out there is the patient zero of low-rise jeans. The trick is finding her. In the '90s, a cottage industry of cool-hunters sprung forward claiming to be fortune tellers of teen taste. Some were right. Most were wrong. So these days most fashion houses go right to the source.

Sophie May: Every time somebody copies me, which I'm, you know, flattered if they do, I change it.

Bill Weir: Sophie May is a ninth grader who loves to shop. But unlike most ninth graders she rides a corporate stretch Hummer to the mall where designers and consultants study her every move.

Teen Observer: This is an "It Girl Challenge." I think you can do it. Ready, set, go.

Bill Weir: Sophie May is one in an army of "Teen Vogue It Girls."

Teen Observer: You're an It Girl. Okay.

Bill Weir: If the new Betsey Johnson cell phone is going to sweep the nation, it will probably have to sweep them first. Which is how 16 year olds get into swank New York parties.

Teen Vogue It Girl: I can walk into school and say, "look what I've got." And no one can say, "oh yeah, me too."

Teen Observer: They are influencers. And the fact is that when you reach one, you reach so many other teen girls.

Teen Vogue It Girl: I think it's cute and it's girly and it's fun.

Bill Weir: At the ultra-hip Kitson Boutique in Los Angeles, they have a much more efficient way of reaching teen girls. I'm fascinated by why this is the hat of the moment.

Sara Giller: Pretty simple. Lindsay Lohan wore it. Those kurtz hats were not doing very well at all. And Lindsay Lohan came in to the store with her friend Paris Hilton, put one on and was seen walking out of the store and photographed in it and it went like crazy. Like hot cakes.

Bill Weir: So did she wear it because it was cool or is it cool because she wore it? Oh, my head hurts. Either way, it's only a matter of time before this trend goes the way of von Dutch. When do you know that a trend has jumped the shark?

Trend-Watcher: When it goes onto your grandma. Nothing against grandmas. But when grandmas are wearing it you say, hmm, probably time to move on.

Bill Weir: Oh, but don't be so sure. Remember our It Girls?

Sophie May: Actually my first pair of moccasins was for my grandma.

Teen Vogue It Girl: I'd say, half the stuff in my closet is from my grandmother. I have the cutest like cropped blazer and I got it out of my grandmother's closet.

Teen Observer: That's so perfect, it's at-home vintage shopping.

Bill Weir: So there you go. If the granny look sweeps the nation next season you can say you saw it here first. And by the way, if you want to know the power of the teenage consumer, American teens spent $124 billion last year.

Kate Snow: Is that right? Whoa.

Bill Weir: They get the credit cards at the cradle these days.

Kate Snow: Yeah, fascinating piece.

UNIT 5: TUNE IN TO TV

Baby TV
1:48 minutes

Lisa Stark: *Sesame Street* is a favorite with Caroline Mansfield and her kids. Mansfield likes the idea that this well-known company has now developed DVDs for the under-two set.

Carolyn Mansfield: There is a guilt factor. But at least you can know that the content is something that you approve of.

Lisa Stark: The new DVDs joined an explosion of videos for infants, which have come under attack. The American Academy of Pediatrics recommended no TV for those under age 2.

Dr. Alvin Poussaint: I think they're using all these babies right now, encouraging them to watch television. They're using them as guinea pigs in a kind of uncontrolled experiment.

Lisa Stark: But the no-TV recommendation is not based on studies of television programming. And the reality is 68 percent of those under age 2 spend more than two hours a day in front of a screen. The nonprofit Sesame Workshop says it wanted to provide parents and kids with a better option, focusing on child/adult interaction.

Rosemarie Truglio: It's one thing to say to parents "get on the floor, do more with your kid."

But where are they getting the information about how to do more of this? And that's what this DVD is all about.

Lisa Stark: Scientists say there's not enough research on how television affects the very young.

Sandra Calvert: Some of the techniques that work with very young kids are repeating it, showing it several times. And basically, having adults sometimes help interpret, interact with their children.

Lisa Stark: What all the experts agree on, children who watch TV should be with an adult. And the best way to learn is still interactive play, not in front of the television. Lisa Stark, ABC News, Washington.

UNIT 6: SUPERSTITIONS

The Pharaoh's Curse
2:56 minutes

Charles Gibson: Our *Good Morning America* exclusive world event, "The Secrets of Tutankhamen, The Mummy Returns," continues now with the most mysterious part of the tale of Tut, which is the curse of the pharaohs.

And so, we go live to the land of the pyramids for answers, and to ABC's David Wright, who is here with such a beautiful, beautiful backdrop.

David Wright: Charlie, it is an amazing place to be. One of the seven wonders of the world and you can really see why. The great pyramid here in Giza was actually the tallest building in the world until they built the Eiffel Tower just over a century ago. These pyramids have stood for more than 4,000 years. A lot of legends are associated with them, including the curse of the pharaoh. And to put it into context, it's sort of like the, the feeling that many Red Sox fans used to have until last year, and that many Chicago Cubs fans still have. The curse, kind of silly, but then again, bad stuff keeps happening.

Actor 1: Death, eternal punishment for anyone who opens this casket. Good heavens, what a terrible curse.

Actor 2: Well, let's see what's inside.

Actor 1: Wait.

David Wright: The year was 1922. A determined archaeologist named Howard Carter had spent five long years in the Valley of the Kings, searching for Tutankhamen's tomb. The British nobleman who was paying the bills got fed up. Lord Carnarvon gave Carter one last chance. And on November 22nd, 1922, success. Word of the extraordinary treasures circled the globe, but that very day, Carter's good luck canary was eaten by a cobra, the first of many bad omens. Within six months, Lord Carnarvon was dead, infected by a mosquito bite. It was said that all the lights in Cairo went out the moment he died. And his own son reported that the earl's dog, home in England, howled mournfully and then died, too. Whispers of a curse began in earnest, fueling popular imagination. Newspapers, books, and movies picked up the story. Workers, visitors, and translators mysteriously died. An Egyptian prince murdered his wife in London. Every death, every misfortune, attributed to the curse of the pharaohs. So, is there a curse protecting King Tut's tomb? Most Egyptologists say no.

Dr. Zahi Hawass: If you close this tomb for 3,000 years, and there's a mummy inside this tomb, and you open, and you enter, the room will contain germs that you cannot see. It can hit people.

David Wright: Microbes or the mummy's curse? We may never know for sure.

David Wright: It is like the secret of the Sphinx. A riddle that's been kept for 4,500 years. Charlie?

Charles Gibson: All right. David Wright, thanks very much.

UNIT 7: OUR FRAGILE PLANET

The Eagles Return
2:01 minutes

Ned Potter: Thomas Jefferson called the bird "a free spirit, high-soaring and courageous." But it has been a battle to bring it back from the edge.

Peter Nye: Suddenly, our public attitude turned around completely. And we said, wait a minute. This is our national emblem and it means something to us, and we should give it some special treatment.

Ned Potter: Peter Nye heads New York state's endangered species unit. He goes to great lengths, and heights, to make sure their numbers keep growing. He climbs into treetops to check their nests and make sure their offspring are healthy. Forty years ago, the birds were not healthy at all; expanding suburbs destroyed their nesting areas. Pesticides destroyed their eggs. But today, the Interior Department says the number of birds is soaring. It says the Endangered Species Act has done its job, protecting the birds from human interference. And now, the department says it is time for a change.

Craig Manson: The Bald Eagle no longer needs the protection of the Endangered Species Act because it is no longer threatened or endangered.

Ned Potter: The administration would like to remove the birds from the threatened-species list, by the end of the year if possible.

Michael Bean: The job of trying to recover endangered species is a task that is within our grasp. It is not beyond our grasp.

Ned Potter: Some people are worried about that. They say the birds' habitats are still being cut down, that bad chemicals are still out there. In other words, that it is too early to declare victory.

Roger Schlikeisen: There may be a few areas, including California, where the population hasn't really recovered and now has declined.

Ned Potter: But for Peter Nye in New York, a life's work seems to be paying off.

Peter Nye: It's definitely a source of pride and a success story. And it's nice to see it come to fruition.

Ned Potter: When things were at their worst, there was a single eagle's nest in New York state. Today, Nye says, there are 80. Ned Potter, ABC News, New York.

UNIT 8: LIVING A LONG LIFE

Longevity Gene?
2:14 minutes

Lisa Stark: Neddine Parker is up by 7:00 A.M. to have breakfast. After her morning exercises and chores, she drives to the local hospital, where she volunteers.

Neddine Parker: She's a cutie.

Lisa Stark: What makes this so extraordinary is that Neddine is 104 years old.

Neddine Parker: I don't know why I'm still here.

Lisa Stark: Dr. Thomas Perls is trying to figure that out. He studies these superhuman centenarians.

Dr. Thomas Perls: It's a bit like winning the lottery. You've got to get the right numbers and the right combination.

Lisa Stark: Researchers say about 30 percent of aging is genetic. And for those who get to extreme old ages, family history may play an even more important role.

Ruben Landau's mother lived to 100. He is nearly 102, and still practices law.

Ruben Landau: I enjoy it.

Lisa Stark: Both Landau and Parker take few medications, have no major illnesses. Dr. Perls has found that many centenarians lack a certain gene, E-4, that's associated with an increased risk of heart disease and Alzheimer's. One study found the gene is in 29 percent of young men, but only 15 percent of centenarians. Perls is also trying to determine if those who reach 100 have some type of protective gene, one that helps them survive what might kill other people. Parker, for example, smoked until she was 100. And had a stroke at 89.

Neddine Parker: Slight stroke. But I wasn't even aware of it.

Lisa Stark: Researchers are also finding that children of centenarians have a 60 percent reduced rate of heart disease, diabetes, stroke, and high blood pressure. The hope? That one day all this genetic research will lead to drugs that can slow the aging process.

But living into your hundreds isn't just genetics. About 70 percent of aging successfully has to do with environment and behavior.

Landau watches what he eats, and exercises his body and mind every day.

Ruben Landau: I feel fine.

Dr. Thomas Perls: People still have to do some of the things right to still get to very old age.

Lisa Stark: So, it's not just the cards you're dealt, but how you play the hand. Lisa Stark, ABC News, Boston.